HOW POWERPOINT MAKES YOU STUPID

Also by Franck Frommer

Jean-Patrick Manchette: Le récit d'un engagement manqué

HOW POWERPOINT MAKES YOU STUPID

The Faulty Causality, Sloppy Logic,
Decontextualized Data,
and Seductive Showmanship
That Have Taken Over Our Thinking

FRANCK FROMMER

Translated from the French by George Holoch

The New Press gratefully acknowledges the Florence Gould Foundation for supporting the publication of this book.

First published as *La pensée PowerPoint: Enquête sur ce logiciel qui rend stupide* by La
 Découverte, Paris, 2010
Published in the United States by The New Press, New York, 2012
Distributed by Perseus Distribution

LIBRARY OF CONGRESS CATALOGING-IN-PUBLICATION DATA

Frommer, Franck.
 [Pensée Powerpoint. English]
 How PowerPoint makes you stupid : the faulty causality, sloppy logic,
decontextualized data, and seductive showmanship that have taken over our
thinking / Franck Frommer ; translated from the French by George Holoch.
  p. cm.
 Includes bibliographical references and index.
 ISBN 978-1-59558-702-2 (hardback)
1. Microsoft PowerPoint (Computer file)--Social aspects. I. Title.
 HM851.F7813 2012
 005.5'8--dc23
                           2011033975

The New Press was established in 1990 as a not-for-profit alternative to the large, commercial publishing houses currently dominating the book publishing industry. The New Press operates in the public interest rather than for private gain, and is committed to publishing, in innovative ways, works of educational, cultural, and community value that are often deemed insufficiently profitable.

www.thenewpress.com

Composition by the Influx House
This book was set in Janson Text

Printed in the United States of America

10 9 8 7 6 5 4 3 2 1

CONTENTS

ACKNOWLEDGMENTS

I would like to give my warm thanks to all the men and women, experts or novices, creative or pragmatic, regular or occasional users, amateurs or professionals from very different sectors, who have accompanied me throughout this study. Without their thoughts and observations, my understanding of this powerful medium would not have been possible. They were enthusiastic in thinking about a tool of which they made constant—and almost mechanical—use in their daily life. It is refreshing to remark how many of these exchanges stimulated debates, brain waves, and fruitful hypotheses. PowerPoint leaves no one indifferent. For the sake of convenience and to avoid any embarrassment or unequal treatment, no last names are given and first names have been changed. Everyone quoted will recognize him- or herself. I would again like to thank all of them for their generous insights.

I would finally like to particularly thank Hugues Jallon, who encouraged me to carry out this study and provided invaluable help throughout its writing, as well as Véronique F., an intransigent reader who bore with great patience the slow maturation of this work, and Jeanne for her linguistic assistance.

INTRODUCTION

In 2001, Microsoft estimated that 30 million PowerPoint presentations were given every day. The company now estimates
that 500 million people use the program. "The 2007 edition of
Microsoft Office Home and Student, which includes PowerPoint,
has been the best-selling software in the United States consumer
market since 2008. . . . In France, sales have doubled in the last
18 months," according to a triumphant Microsoft press release
at the end of 2009 announcing the coming launch of the 2010
version of the program.

Over the last ten years, PowerPoint, the computer-assisted
presentation program by Microsoft, has become the indispensable medium for any oral presentation, from small office meetings to university lecture halls and major ad campaigns. Seldom
has a commercial device exercised such dominance on the principal forms of collective communication represented by oral
presentations and meetings. Even such "sacred" places as court-
rooms and churches are now theaters of slide projections: it is
possible to re-create a crime scene in court, and any preacher
can rely on PowerPoint to enliven his sermons.

In the beginning, there was an ingenious program created in

the 1980s by the first of the West Coast geeks. This precursor made it possible to produce organized, easy-to-use multimedia presentations simply and quickly. They could include animation, illustrations, photographs, sound, video, and hypertext links. It was already a complete and universal tool "to create dynamic and snappy presentations," as the official site for PowerPoint still asserts.

At first, PowerPoint was intended primarily for office meetings or for the presentation of products and services. As it improved over time, the program acquired graphic and multimedia capabilities that opened the door to new territories: technological innovation made it possible with a few clicks and bullet points to adapt and simplify centuries of rhetorical art.

A tool for demonstrations, used for commercial or professional communication purposes, PowerPoint has invented a comprehensive rhetorical apparatus in which all the classic techniques of argument have been cleverly absorbed or transformed. It offers a particular form of expression for speech and proposes a kind of exhibition that has profoundly changed interpersonal relationships.

HOW A COMPUTER PROGRAM EDITS OUR THOUGHTS

"PowerPoint makes us stupid." This is what Marine General James N. Mattis declared at a military conference (in a speech given without PowerPoint) in North Carolina in April 2010. The article in the *New York Times* reporting the remark revealed the pervasive role the software was playing in the American armed forces. It reached the point that the then head of American and NATO forces in Afghanistan, General Stanley A. McChrystal, accused PowerPoint of having become the U.S. Army's principal enemy, nothing less.[1]

PowerPoint experienced phenomenal success as soon as it was released in 1987, but criticisms did not appear until the early 2000s. A first investigation, as serious as it was sarcastic, "Can a Software Package Edit Our Thoughts?" was published in the *New Yorker* in 2001. In it, Ian Parker relates, with many anecdotes, the meteoric rise of PowerPoint and already notes its ubiquity in places like schools and the military. He recounts that some bosses have already prohibited the use of PowerPoint in their companies. Ian Parker was one of the first to draw attention to the PowerPoint world:

> In the glow of a PowerPoint show, the world is condensed, simplified, and smoothed over—yet bright and hyperreal—like the cityscape background in a PlayStation motor race. PowerPoint is strangely adept at disguising the fragile foundations of a proposal, the emptiness of a business plan; usually the audience is respectfully still (only venture capitalists dare to dictate the pace of someone else's slide show), and with the visual distraction of a dancing pie chart, a speaker can quickly move past the laughable flaw in his argument.[2]

The most savage attack came two years later in an essay by Edward Tufte, *The Cognitive Style of PowerPoint*.[3] In twenty-eight illustrated pages, with a tone and examples that are as mischievous as its dissection and analysis are rigorous, this American expert in graphic communication demolishes the software, relying in particular on NASA documents used during the space shuttle *Columbia* accident in 2003. Dissecting a single slide, Tufte takes apart the graphic and discursive mechanisms that helped to obscure essential information that could have sounded the alarm about the possibility of an accident. A few months later, the investigating committee's report took harshly critical note of NASA's recurrent use of PowerPoint and its glaring inadequacy in dealing with this kind of information.

Tufte uses other, less tragic examples that nonetheless confirm the risks of abuse or misuse of this kind of prop:

> PowerPoint's convenience for some presenters is costly to the content and the audience. These costs arise from the *cognitive style characteristic of the standard default PP presentation*: foreshortening of evidence and thought, low spatial resolution, an intensely hierarchical single-path structure as the model for organizing every type of content, breaking up narratives and data into slides and minimal fragments, rapid temporal sequencing of thin information rather than focused spatial analysis, conspicuous chartjunk and PP Phluff, branding of slides with logotypes, a preoccupation with format not content, incompetent design for data graphics and tables, and a smirky commercialism that turns information into a sales pitch and presenters into marketeers.[4]

The virulence of the argument should not make us forget that the literature on PowerPoint is still largely made up of technical advice manuals to prepare beautiful presentations, more serious studies on its pedagogical effectiveness, and timid critiques intended primarily to sell the services of smarter PowerPoint designers. Yet the feeling that PowerPoint induces a formatting of thought by means of the expected combination of different media is finding traction, particularly in American colleges and universities, where the software is ubiquitous. In 2006, an expert even amused himself by calculating the savings a bank like Citigroup, then one of the largest in the world, would make by cutting down the time given to meetings and the preparation of bad PowerPoint presentations. He came up with $47 million.

FROM NASA TO NURSERY SCHOOL

Before going on, it should be said that this book does not provide advice on how to make slides more readable and attractive,
nor is it a guide for composing good titles, finding good pictures, enlivening a meeting, or speaking in public.

This book tries to understand and evaluate the devastating
effects of what I have chosen to call PowerPoint thinking. It
tries to understand how what started out as a simple medium
accompanied, accelerated, and sometimes initiated fundamental changes in business and in the transmission of information
and knowledge. It tries to grasp the ideological underpinnings
of this new medium—as we know, a medium is never neutral—
and its growing dominance over the way thought is expressed
and, most important, conceived in contemporary society.

The invention of PowerPoint, described in the first chapter of
the book, came at a key moment in our recent history, the 1980s,
when the business world was undergoing profound changes in
organization and ways of cooperating: hierarchy was given up in
favor of flat organization, authority gave way to autonomy, and
following orders was replaced by creativity. Companies increasingly relied on the universal method of management by project.
And projects meant exchanges, discussions, meetings, and so on:
PowerPoint soon became the indispensable tool for both large
and small projects (chapter 2).

Chapters 3, 4, and 5 analyze the forms of discourse, graphics,
and staging implemented in PowerPoint. A powerful and complete medium, PowerPoint makes it possible to bring together
discourse, images, and spectacle. Because of its technical limitations, the software has established a specific grammar that makes
necessary simplified statements, limited syntactical forms, and

discursive procedures that usually amount to neutralizing anything out of the ordinary. Images seem to have contradictory functions: an argument from authority in the case of outlines and diagrams, they are also intended to decorate, illustrate, or amuse the audience. They focus as well as distract the attention. As for the art of oratory itself, it is hardly different from that of an actor in the best case or a clown in the worst. PowerPoint has created a specific genre and has been able to find stars to proclaim its value loud and clear, especially its way of magnifying the medium in technical terms.

The last three chapters give an account of the general contamination of all areas by PowerPoint. This epidemic accelerated in the 2000s with the massive outsourcing of expertise to consultants in many areas of activity. At first limited to technical and financial matters, the gradual invasion of consultants fostered the proliferation of their primary mode of communication: the slide. Companies built strategies and organizations on the basis of ever more meticulous and animated matrices and pie charts.

Then these devices gradually infiltrated into the public sphere and the administration. The army was the sector probably most overwhelmed by the infection, as indicated by the numerous interventions of the American service chiefs. But states as well, their administrative and public services, driven by management models from private enterprise, also fell under the spell of bullet points. Health and human resources, universities and schools, practically no sector seems to have escaped contamination.

HOW POWERPOINT MAKES YOU STUPID

1

THE INVENTION
OF A UNIVERSAL MEDIUM

➡

"In the early 1980s, when we were preparing presentations for salesmen in the field, for conferences intended for prospects or customers, we used an overhead projector and transparencies: we typed the text on a typewriter and photocopied it onto transparencies. Then we put the transparency, in black and white, on an overhead projector, and we projected it on a wall or a screen. We could add sketches in real time with a marker."

Frédéric R. has worked for more than thirty years in the sales division of a major French insurance company. He worked on the design and preparation of all kinds of presentations, for training salesmen, unveiling a new product, enlivening a conference with customers or a project meeting, and so on. A former computer programmer, he went through all the changes of the 1970s and 1980s in presentation hardware and software. Today he talks about it with nostalgia and a bit of astonishment when he considers the path that has been traveled.

THE "PLASTIC" YEARS

The use of graphic presentations in work meetings does not date from the invention of the transparency and the whole office arsenal of the 1960s. It started becoming popular in the United States in the 1920s. At the time, formal presentations with visual props were not yet in common use. The preference was for oral presentations with notes and informal discussions.

The tendency to produce visuals, graphics, and tables of numbers grew out of an underlying movement in American management in the 1910s and 1920s that involved recording and comparing company data.[1] Firms were growing exponentially, and their forms of organization were evolving. The multidivisional form with autonomous branches gradually became the rule, replacing the functional and hierarchical approach.

The concept of multidivisional form was devised by the economist and business historian Alfred Chandler. In one of his best known books, *The Visible Hand*, on the basis of an analysis of American economic history, Chandler concludes that the "visible hand" of managers of modern companies has replaced the "invisible hand" of the market that dominated traditional small business.[2] He shows how large American companies, such as Standard Oil, General Electric, and DuPont, integrated all the functions needed to supply a product or service: design, production, distribution, and so on. Known as a multidivisional firm, this organization became the model of the largest companies, particularly in America.[3]

These more "horizontal" organizations had to have means of communication for the exchange and comparison of data. And it soon turned out that graphic presentations had the capacity to persuade management clearly and in a generalized way.

To meet this need, the managers of one of the industrial giants of the period, DuPont, began using this kind of presentation in the 1920s in their annual top management meetings to exchange ideas, resolve problems, and make decisions.[4] The company went so far as to create a chart room set aside for these presentation materials:[5]

> Sometime between 1919 and 1922 a special chart-viewing room was designed for meetings of the firm's Executive Committee. The room had 350 charts, updated regularly, displaying various aspects of the return-on-investment data for DuPont's multiple divisions. As the committee members deliberated, responsible division members would be called in to explain any anomalies in the charts.[6]

In 1914, Willard C. Brinton published the first manual on graphic presentation.[7] Although his book was primarily concerned with the use of graphs as tools for analysis, it also dealt with the question of visual aids in presentations, notably the projection of transparencies to accompany a presentation, thereby demonstrating the value of graphs as a means of communication for management.

After World War II, the needs of the military and the proliferation of American government agencies drove a growing demand for means of exchanging and sharing information. The army, which had significant research funding at its disposal, adopted effective technologies for intelligence gathering and transmission. Presentations with visual aids became more and more frequent, using the media available at the time: including modern paperboard,[8] the more traditional blackboard, and classic transparency projections, especially 3M transparencies.

Who could have predicted that the abrasives maker Minnesota Mining & Manufacturing (3M), founded in 1902, would become one of the most innovative companies of the twentieth century? From sandpaper to Scotch tape, from Post-it notes to film for overhead projectors, from Tartan tape to magnetic tape, from offset printing plates to infrared photocopiers, from fabric protection treatment to scouring pads, the history of 3M is punctuated with inventions that have often transformed the practice of certain professions, notably computing and graphics, but also and above all the daily lives of millions of people around the world, in offices and factories as well as kitchens and bathrooms.

In the 1950s, 3M developed an interest in photographic products, particularly overhead projection systems. Roger Appledorn, a young physicist working on the thermofax, was challenged by his mentor and boss, Emil Grieshaber, to produce transparencies onto which color images could be copied and that could then be projected onto a screen. The young researcher succeeded, and a huge market opened up: one of the first customers was the Strategic Air Command. Established in 1946, this division of the U.S. Air Force, whose purpose was to organize strategic bombing units armed with atomic weapons, used "about 20,000 sheets of film each month in their war room."[9]

A war room was originally an operations room used for coordinating military actions at the highest strategic level and bringing together members of the government assigned to security questions and the heads of all the service branches of the armed forces. In fact, the war room has turned out to be an excellent tool for sharing and exchanging information on any major projects. Some companies have modified the concept for their purposes, creating war rooms to analyze the market, study the launch of new products, or examine proposed acquisitions, reorganizations, and invitations to bid.[10]

The company soon understood that this was a promising market. It had been subcontracting out the manufacture of overhead projectors but now decided to produce everything itself, projectors and film, so it could sell the entire line of products. But the machines turned out to be too expensive, noisy, and cumbersome, and they produced too much heat. They were a commercial failure. Adaptations improved the projector, but customers wanted one that was as small as a briefcase and easier to use.

It was not until January 15, 1962, that Appledorn's team presented the first overhead projector with a new Fresnel lens. Much cheaper to make and easier to use, the product had triumphed by August 1962: "Schools wanted them. Businesses needed them; so did government agencies. The product became the basis for the Visual Products Division within a few years."[11]

Already widely used by all American security forces, including the army, police,[12] and CIA, transparencies gradually penetrated into sports for training in football or baseball and into schools and universities. These projection systems did not fully enter the life of business enterprises until the mid-1960s. Often limited by the small fonts of typewriters and the limited graphic skills of assistants, notably in the use of Letraset,[13] the transparencies produced at the time have a shoddy look and did not always have the expected success.

To remedy these difficulties, by the 1970s companies were calling on the expertise of graphic designers to create customized transparency modules according to specific needs: conferences, training, seminars, and so on. It was then possible to put together libraries of good-quality transparencies designed and manufactured by graphic designers and stored in file folders. According to a former consultant of a major French study institute, "We used many transparencies, which in the best cases, were created on the basis of photocopies with tables and diagrams. There were also transparencies on which we could write directly and quickly with markers. We could redo a summary, add data, and write recommendations or last-minute details." The medium allowed for more interaction and participation, which would no longer be the case with the slide show, the ancestor of PowerPoint.

Transparencies were the basic material for any internal business presentation, but universities, laboratories, and government agencies favored 35-millimeter photographic slides for higher-quality exhibitions intended for a public audience, particularly in commercial and advertising presentations. Slides were made on computers and then developed like photographs.

From 1975 to 1985, the number of projectors sold annually in the United States rose from about 50,000 to more than 120,000.[14] By then a few rules of presentation had begun to circulate. Transparencies were presented vertically in page or portrait mode, because presentations still consisted mainly of text and had very few illustrations. The first transparencies were often merely sections of long notes embellished with a few tables and graphs that were simply photocopied and reproduced on a screen. For purposes of organization and efficiency, and above all because these media became essential aids for the organization of meetings, designers increasingly shortened the texts to make them more summary in nature and gradually moved toward the notorious PowerPoint bullet list, with indentation to indicate subcategories, that became, in landscape mode, the standard horizontal format of all presentations.

Presenters used manual tricks to enliven their presentations, such as gradually revealing the information by covering a portion of the transparency with a blank sheet of paper and sliding it up or down, or superposing transparencies on one another to show drawings or graphs. Each regular user had his own techniques to make projections more playful and dynamic. According to a former trainer who worked for many years for Cegos, a leading European professional training company:

In the beginning, we used them for two purposes: either for official presentations with transparencies designed in color or for working meetings and training sessions. Then we used blank transparencies set on overhead projectors on which we wrote directly with markers as though it was a blackboard. It very handily replaced paperboard: we could present a sketch, write on it directly to supplement it, and erase certain elements. We had batteries of prepared kits: we didn't create anything ourselves, and it was already very tightly organized.

But with the nascent expansion of computing, the physical media of presentation would gradually give way to weightless and much more powerful media.

THEN CAME IT . . .

The first mass-market microcomputers, PCs and Macintoshes, appeared on the market in the first half of the 1980s. They were large, heavy, and expensive, but some were transportable.

The microcomputer had in fact seen the light in France about ten years earlier. In 1972, in response to a commission from the National Institute of Agricultural Research (INRA), a French engineer named André Tuong, who had founded the computer company R2E a year earlier, designed the Micral. As large as the central unit of an office computer, this "micro" had neither a screen nor a keyboard, and data entry was performed using switches. Five hundred Micrals were produced in 1972 and sold for about 8500 francs ($1,750). The June 1973 issue of the American magazine *Byte* designated the Micral as a "microcomputer." This precursor did not have the success anticipated and was used primarily for the automation of highway toll booths.

The microcomputer market was really launched in July 1974 by Sun's 8080 microprocessor, which made it possible to design the Altair, the first micro in the history of computers that was accessible to everyone. What was unknown at the time was that this invention would strike a severe blow against the "large systems" computing that had been established in companies since the 1960s:

> The first service businesses to become computerized were banks and insurance companies; in other sectors, the first uses were in accounting, payroll, and inventory management. This changed the physical conditions of work: in the 1960s, employees spent part of their time perforating cards and going over lists; then, in the 1970s and 1980s, terminals were installed, replaced by networked micro-computers in the 1990s. At each stage, the ergonomics were modified as well as the possibilities offered to the user.[15]

The advent of microcomputing in business had a considerable influence on the organization of work, particularly on the omnipotence of information systems. In the 1960s, computer systems were still highly centralized and technically complex. Users had to connect to the system through passive terminals to access their documents or applications. The uses of the computer were restricted to only those operations permitted by the machine.

With the microcomputer, the horizon expanded: all the tools, notably those involved in office automation, were accessible independently and without limitation. Terminals were no longer passive but permitted both the storage and the processing of data through applications accessible from a distance or integrated into the microcomputer. Employees had the benefit of more accessible, lighter, and more mobile computers, which gave them more autonomy.

This microcomputer revolution accelerated between 1975 and 1985: Microsoft was established in 1976; Commodore and Apple both launched microcomputers in 1977. The mastodon IBM decided to produce its first machine in 1981.[16] Compaq marketed the first portable microcomputer, weighing over thirty pounds, in 1982, and Apple sold its first Macintosh in 1984. Increasing numbers of companies began to see the advantages of these lighter systems over large centralized ones. The dynamic grew in the course of the 1980s, thanks to a prodigious revolution in material that was made ever lighter and easier to use.[17]

In the early 1980s, before the story of PowerPoint began, it became increasingly necessary for departments, divisions, or offices to communicate with each other: the sales force started talking to production workers, who talked to computing services, who started meeting with marketing personnel. This period produced profound changes in the ways companies operated. From a highly rationalized, compartmentalized, and hierarchical operation, a legacy of the Frederick Taylor model, organization became more decentralized, autonomous, networked, and mobile, under the joint influence of new theories of management coming from both the United States and Japan.

The spread of automated office tools created a profound transformation in the most common work habits: "Now contained in software programs rather than command structures, the split between execution and conception concretizes, in a twofold monopoly of knowledge and decision-making, the Taylorist principles of the organization of work. Computing, and office automation more generally, has asserted itself as a technology of power."[18] Previously, each department had been turned inward: each one spoke its own language, with its own concepts, its numbers, its values, its "culture," and so on. What brought them together was the product they were selling and especially the mass of information that each one had to process in its area and then share with the others.

Thus, thanks to the coordinated attraction of the multidivisional firm and management by projects or by objectives,[19] meetings with presentation devices intended to provide information from the bottom up (reporting and performance indicators, idea exchange on projects, project committee and project review, steering committee) or from the top down (management committee, strategic plan) became an essential resource for the organization.

In the same period, the growing dominance of marketing, with the mantra "The customer is king," and of a consumerism that had become the only universal value perfected the formatting of exchanges and communication in companies, making "presentation" a must for any interlocutor in economic and social life.

This was a profound change. According to Norbert Alter, in the first half of the 1980s, "the information sector, which accounts for the work of production, processing, and diffusion of information, compared to all other sectors combined, amounts to more than half the active population in developed countries. . . . Beyond traditional distinctions between agriculture, industry, and services, a new activity has appeared, that is already or will soon be in the majority: the work on languages and signs."[20] This analysis chimes with that of Bill Clinton's Secretary of Labor, Robert Reich, in an influential book on "symbolic analysts," advisers, communicators, experts, consultants, all the winners of globalization who are dominant today in organizations around the world in contrast to producers, clerks, and other holders of insecure jobs.[21]

The processing of information, mastery over all its forms, has become the alpha and omega of every organization. In some financial establishments, for example, this permanent oversight of information, essential in production mechanisms from the creation of a product to customer relations, has led the company to give more and more power to the tools and applications placed under the responsibility of the information systems divisions (ISD). Today it is futile, for example, to consider launching a new product in any sector without having first studied its feasibility in terms of the information system: from design through manufacture to management, the entire chain is dependent on computer processing.

Techniques, management methods, tools, all the day-to-day habits of the company are practically—indeed symbolically in the very way of speaking—"contaminated" by information technology, which has the consequence of changing the role, the task, and the expertise of everyone. There has been a shift from already acquired qualifications to the acquisition of new skills: what used to be the privilege of management—the mastery of tools and language—has become that of subordinates, whereas some in management have begun to prepare their own documents without using secretaries. In the case of word processing, there has been a reversal of roles: managers are forced to bring texts to be typed, formatted, and formalized to someone who masters a tool that they do not. "That made possible the parallel professionalization of the consultant and the assistants whose work that often was. At the time, heads of companies had an increasing tendency, out of a concern for economy, to have managers carry out tasks that used to devolve on secretaries," according to Bruno R., a former consultant to a major French study institute. This tendency was magnified in the 1990s: many companies engaged in a vast movement of "autonomization" of their managers to the detriment of assistants, who even virtually disappeared from some companies.

The "technological" graft succeeded; from now on, knowledge acquired at school and official qualifications were not enough. It was better to be completely independent at one's workplace, having acquired the requisite skills, mastering everything from design to execution.

> There is an underlying shift from 'rational legal' authority, based on the attribution of roles through rules, toward an authority of experts over other experts defined by their actions in the production process: one is judged not on status but by what one does. . . . The place and number of "knowledge workers" or "professional managers" . . . who are defined by their own work, not by supervising the work of others, is growing at the expense of middle management who seem to be the unproductive personnel in the organization of knowledge.[22]

Thus the sharing of information—still a major question of power for the hierarchy in some companies—in ordinary work meetings has been completely changed by the contribution of new tools fostering collective creation, exchange, collaboration, and debate. Meetings with "predigested" information that are episodic and without discussion are a thing of the past.

If the organization of work involves more interdependence and sharing, it is essential that everyone provide homogeneous data accessible at every operational level of the hierarchy. If new work values have appeared, such as autonomy and creativity, in practice the employee must above all be versatile and able to do everything alone, an incessant demand from company heads, in the name of the sacrosanct mobility and permanent adaptation to change.

But this movement toward empowerment has taken place gradually, as indicated, for example, by a consultant who is now a freelancer:

In the mid-1990s, reports in Word were typed by secretaries, and one person who had a degree in fine art made our slides. It bored him because he found it not very creative. In another firm where I worked later, there was a Report division, because they produced a lot of them at the time. Then under pressure from clients, we were forced to turn out more and more reports in the form of slides.

A former engineer, Patrick M., started out with a consulting firm in the 1980s. He was soon drawn to automated office tools:

When I started out with Andersen [now Accenture], we were far from computers: we used pens, pencils, paper, faxes. Secretaries still did word processing "by the mile" on old passive terminals. We were far from computer tools for presentation. We commonly used transparencies; we transposed primitive sketches onto transparencies and then showed them on the wall with a Barco overhead projector.[23]

For many of these consultants, the real revolution was the advent of the Macintosh in the 1990s. It enabled them to bypass secretaries for word processing. Consultants trained themselves quickly and were soon operational. Macs at first were shared and then gradually distributed individually. The first PCs with Windows appeared around 1996, responding to the desire of companies to generalize personal computing, particularly in consulting companies, where the computer became an everyday tool for all consultants. It was a question of cost and efficiency: the autonomous consultant was a source of savings.

... AND POWERPOINT

The deployment and spread of microcomputers also implies the development of software enabling the machines to operate and be "intelligent." With respect to presentation and graphic creation, the software on offer followed the exponential development of the hardware.

In the early 1990s, the pioneers used various programs, including CA-Cricket Presents,[24] which made it possible to create the equivalent of transparencies, subsequently shown through an interface between the Macintosh and the overhead projector. Around the same time, the very first video projectors appeared. The highest performing had a power of 500 lumens, weighed over twenty pounds, and looked like cannons.[25] The room had to be completely dark if anything was to be visible on the screen.

For the promotion of his commercial activities, Frédéric R. sought the help of a graphic designer:

> We used Adobe Illustrator [developed on Macintosh in 1985]: I operated the program following his design advice. We identified a scenario—training module, product promotion, retirement program, activities seminar—on the basis of basically identical language. At the time, I could almost create my own presentations by myself for an audience of two hundred.

Under Windows 95, the world of physical media—the slide— is increasingly left behind in favor of the entirely digital, after the advent in 1992 of animation software with impressive capabilities, such as Director or Persuasion, seemingly the last word in interactive and sequential software for making graphs, picto-grams, and animation.

And then PowerPoint came.

The first version of the program was released in April 1987 and operated only on Macintosh. It made it possible to create black-and-white transparencies that could be printed and dis-tributed to the audience. Version 2.0 for Mac was released in May 1988, and for Windows two years later. This version could produce professional 35 mm color slides designed to be projected in large auditoriums.

According to Mireille G., a pioneer in this area in France in a major financial enterprise,

> By 1992, we made available for those who wanted it a station for preparing multimedia documents: the station consisted of a Mac, a digital photo apparatus, a scanner, a color printer, and a program called Slidewriter, which enabled us either to make 35 mm slides or to project directly with a large video projector. Making slides took some time: to make the pictures, send them to the photo lab for making slides, and so on, you had to count on a good twelve hours. There was a high demand at the time, because no one had software for making presentations,

But it was version 3.0, released in the summer of 1992, that made PowerPoint the graphic tool we know today, with color, the possibility of direct transfer to video, the dynamics of the slide show, animation, and the possibility of incorporating other audio or video media. Its creator, Robert Gaskins, recalls:

> The very first public use of a laptop to project video from PowerPoint took place on 25 February 1992, at the Hotel Regina, in the Place des Pyramides, Paris [across from the

Tuileries]. With a laptop casually under my arm, I entered at the back of a ballroom filled with hundreds of Microsoft people from the European, Middle Eastern, and African subsidiaries. I walked through the audience carrying the laptop, up to a podium at the front; there I opened the laptop, and plugged in a video cable on the lectern. I began delivering a presentation to introduce PowerPoint 3.0 for Windows, using PowerPoint 3.0 running on the laptop feeding video out to a projector the size of a refrigerator which put the "video slides" onto a huge screen behind me.[26]

At the time, no one had ever seen a PowerPoint presentation conducted from a laptop, much less used the program to project a video in real time, in color, with animation and transitions. The public, made up primarily of Microsoft personnel, immediately understood how this tool was going to change the company's future. Gaskins explains that he had had to bring his own material from the United States. "Testing and tweaking went on far into the night, but on Tuesday morning, I could 'casually' carry my laptop up to the front, plug in the video cable, and start my PowerPoint." It is no doubt one of the most famous presentations in the history of PowerPoint. As for many technological innovations—as we will see with Steve Jobs and Apple—announcement, presentation, marketing, and promotion could not be contemplated without staging.

Adopted around the world, PowerPoint has received dozens of awards. In 1992, the program had 63 percent of the market for graphic presentation software on Windows and Mac: more than a million licenses were sold, producing annual revenues of $100 million, half from outside the United States. "We were one of the most profitable units at Microsoft, earning an operating profit margin of 48% of revenues (Microsoft's operating margin for the same period was 35%, the software industry average was 11%)," says Gaskins.

After he left, ten years later, in 2003, PowerPoint revenues reached $1 billion annually. PowerPoint was used by 500 million people around the world.

Before 1990 and the creation of Microsoft Office, PowerPoint was sold as a stand-alone product. Two other major Microsoft office products were added to it in 1990: the word processor Word and the spreadsheet Excel. With the success of these three applications, it had become obvious that a single package had to be set up bringing the three products together. Microsoft Office became the number one office tool for many years to come.

BUT WHO INVENTED POWERPOINT?

Predestination or determinism? From a family of salesmen of photographic equipment, Robert Gaskins grew up surrounded by overhead projectors, enlargers, and all the products needed at the time for photography. Like many of his colleagues who "invented" computing in the 1970s, he was a student at the University of California at Berkeley, where he produced pro-grams for Chinese translation and the design of Egyptian hi-eroglyphics. He even invented a machine for creating haikus. Berkeley, Stanford, Silicon Valley: California, the birthplace of Hewlett-Packard, Apple, Sun, and Intel was hacker heaven. According to Michel Volle's history of the microcomputer:

Those hackers had nothing in common with the computer pi-rates of today: They were not pirates, breakers of security codes, makers of viruses: the word "hacker" has only recently taken on that pejorative meaning. In the 1960s, computing was a matter for professionals trained by IBM. Ostentatiously serious, they were dressed in suits with black ties and white shirts. Users were not authorized to approach the machine. But hackers (who were also called hobbyists) demanded the right to understand how the machine worked, to have access to it, to work in real time, and hence to change the way the computer was used. Before them, a computer was a large machine with no screen, no sound card, no word processing, no spreadsheet, no network, and so on. They invented the procedures making possible the introduction of those improvements.[27]

They were the ones who made computers accessible to everyone. They could be found at MIT, AT&T's Bell Labs, Berkeley, and the Palo Alto Research Center (PARC) of Xerox. The major components of the microcomputer were invented in the Xerox laboratories: mouse, graphic interface, drop-down menus, and so on.

When he graduated from Berkeley in 1978, Gaskins went to work for one of the most prestigious research and development labs in the country, Bell Northern Research, located just opposite PARC in Stanford. He conducted research and development in various areas of computing and communications, notably on networks of personal computers, graphic interfaces, digital typesetting, and digital voice-over, and pursued advanced research in public-key encryption systems.

Gaskins speaks of his participation in important strategic meetings to decide on the response to the first personal computer produced by Apple and IBM. He then was appointed head of a European subsidiary and put in charge of a project to create a line of personal computers and servers, hardware and software, designed in nine languages. "Within fourteen months we shipped the first Intel 286–based personal computers in Europe, based on Microsoft system and application software (which was how I came to know Bill Gates)."

In connection with his work, Gaskins saw hundreds of presentations with transparencies, slides, and tables (some done on computers, but most not). Professionally very nomadic, he thought of a possible new application that would enable one to make presentations using personal computers like the Macintosh or the PC. The idea of PowerPoint was beginning to germinate.

As often with technical and scientific inventions, there are those who challenge this version of the story. It turns out that the real inventor is not necessarily the one who filed the patent.

In the course of his investigation of PowerPoint in 2001, Ian Parker met a man named Whitfield Diffie, who acknowledged for the first time his presence at the birth of PowerPoint.

> It was an odd piece of news: as if Lenin had invented the stapler. . . . This is not of great consequence to Diffie, whose reputation in his own field is so high that he is one of the few computer scientists to receive erotically charged fan mail. He said he was "mildly miffed" to have made no money from the PowerPoint connection, but he has no interest in beginning a feud with an old friend. "Bob was the one who had the vision to understand how important it was to the world," he said. "And I didn't."[28]

Who is Bailey Whitfield Diffie, who happened to be in the same lab as Gaskins? A gifted mathematician now in his sixties, Diffie has long gray hair and is a former peacenik. Conducting a small private war against exclusive control by the American government over encryption systems, he revolutionized the world of cryptography in 1976, with his colleagues Martin Hellman and Ralph Merkle, by inventing "asymmetrical cryptography," a precursor of Secure Sockets Layer (SSL) and its successor, Transport Layer Security (TLS), procedures used for secure payments on the Internet.

Diffie was then little concerned with graphic presentations. But the legend is persistent. In 1981, he prepared a presentation for his bosses on the security of telephone systems. To make his lecture more pleasant and to include information not orally transmittable, such as tables and graphs, he had to resign himself, like all his colleagues at the time, to prepare his exposition with 35 mm color slides, the obligatory format for any serious quality presentation but requiring lengthy participation by designers and graphic artists.

To avoid this problem and keep his hands on the document, the ingenious inventor concocted a little program on the basis of graphic tools developed by his Bell Northern colleagues. Then he expanded the method so the page could hold a certain number of frames containing text and images, with space for commentary. He had in fact designed the model for a slide show on paper that he thought he could send to the designers, who would only have to prepare the slides. At the same time, he could also use those slides as the script for his presentation. In a few days' effort—the legend speaks of less than a week—Whitfield Diffie had invented the principles of a program that would become PowerPoint.

In 1982, on his return from a foreign business trip of almost six months, Gaskins noticed that his colleagues were all trying to reproduce slides in Diffie's style to summarize their projects, to make their pitches for financing. But the result was often mediocre. Gaskins now had his idea: create a graphic program able to operate with Windows and Macintosh with which you could create slides.

In 1984, Gaskins left Bell Northern Research and joined

Forethought, a struggling young software company in Sunnyvale in Silicon Valley, as vice president for product development. In 1986, he described his new product, still known as Presenter, and defined his strategy for conquering the market.[29] A few months later, he hired Dennis Austin, a former employee of Burroughs,[30] to design and develop the software. Then it was the turn of Tom Rudkin, a former Intel employee, to direct the work for the future version for Windows. "We raised about $3 million in new money for the re-start from top-tier venture capital investors," says Gaskins. "While we developed PowerPoint, our company operations were simultaneously built up by contract publishing and selling of software belonging to other developers, so that we were ready and able to sell and ship over $1 million worth of PowerPoint on the day of its initial release—unprecedented for a Macintosh application."

MORE AND MORE "MAGICAL"

Three months later, the history of PowerPoint encountered one of its first turning points, an offer from Bill Gates, who wanted to buy the software and make Forethought into a graphic unit of Microsoft located in Silicon Valley.

Bill Gates was persuaded by his associates that this tool could become a major element in tomorrow's automated office. As Gaskins tells it:

> We accepted the offer and became Microsoft's first significant acquisition. The price was $14 million in cash, which returned $12 million to our investors in under three years. I and all the rest of the PowerPoint people, plus many of our other Forethought employees, became Microsoft employees, just a year or so after the Microsoft IPO.

According to Gaskins, a good sign for the acquisition was that whereas other potential purchasers had sent accountants to examine their bank statements, Microsoft had sent a computer expert, Dave Moore, to read the lines of code and question the developers of the newly acquired company. Gaskins congratulated himself after the fact that his company had been able to maintain a surprising degree of organizational independence within a giant like Microsoft. Resolutely autonomous and far from Redmond headquarters, the creator of PowerPoint became the head of Microsoft's Graphics Business Unit. The company grew from seven to nearly one hundred employees, whereas Microsoft in the same period grew from 1,200 to 12,000.

Within a few years and following the development of successive versions, PowerPoint became the world's most popular presentation format, replacing traditional transparencies and photographic slides. Gaskins comments:

> All this was predicted in my strategy documents from the mid-1980s; what was unexpected was that the same hardware would also extend PowerPoint use into university teaching, children's school reports and science fair projects, sermons in churches, super-titles for opera houses, and many other uses that its creators had never imagined.

Gaskins has since changed activities in a novel way, becoming one of the world's major specialists in the concertina, the little accordion used by clowns.[31]

PowerPoint subsequently went through many changes, sometimes unfortunate, according to its inventor—for example, its absorption by the Office package in 1990. In February 1994, version 4.0 of PowerPoint offered a series of ready-to-use templates and illustrations. This application, in principle intended for novice presenters paralyzed in front of a blank page, was called AutoContent Wizard. The developers had designed ready-to-use presentation frames that new users could select with two clicks. The idea seemed so "crazy" that the facetious technicians decided to call it a Wizard, suggesting both magician and expert. Despite the mockery implicit in the name, Microsoft decided to keep it: "a rare example of a product named in outright mockery of its target customers."[32]

This new functionality won approval from thousands of amateurs who had no idea of how to construct a presentation, either a simple lecture or a more graphically sophisticated show. But these pre-written templates also drew gibes from the more expert, who sensed the coming of a kind of normalization of presentations.

They were not entirely wrong: in the 1997 version of PowerPoint, they discovered predefined formats inspired by Dale Carnegie. Carnegie, who had died in 1955, devised a method of personal development based on positive thinking and made it into a lucrative business with the two bestsellers that made him successful: *How to Win Friends and Influence People* and *Public Speaking and Influencing Men in Business*. The methods developed by Carnegie are still taught in training courses around the world, intended particularly for salespeople and managers. It is hardly surprising that the industry of public speaking, oral presentations, and running meetings adapted this new gadget by applying its own recipes for success; they may have been old fashioned, but they had proved themselves.

There is something sourly amusing in recognizing that generations of managers were able to draw inspiration from these ready-to-use models, still present in the 2003 version of the program: "How to Manage a Crisis" and "How to Announce a Restructuring Program," in ten slides that require only the addition of a few numbers and a few recycled messages in managerial jargon.

Gaskins left Microsoft in 1992, and several of his colleagues followed him soon thereafter. In 1993, PowerPoint captured the majority of its market. In 1995, the average user created 4.5 presentations per month. Three years later, the monthly average had risen to nine. As Ian Parker points out, PowerPoint was even showing up in comic strips (particularly in some strips of *Dilbert*, known for its title character, a computer engineer who is the victim of the perverse and Kafkaesque management of his company), in newspaper articles, and in everyday conversation.[33]

In 2001, PowerPoint had 95 percent of the graphic presentation market, and Microsoft estimated that at least 30 million PowerPoint presentations were given every day.

Robert Gaskins, however, was increasingly skeptical about the development of his creation, particularly the AutoContent Wizards that seemed to him to seriously limit the possibilities open to creators of presentations. He also considered some hurriedly concocted preformatted templates to be ridiculous. Finally, he hated animated transitions, particularly with sound, between slides. In one of his initial descriptions of the program, Gaskins had included a sentence that was particularly close to his heart: "Allows the content-originator to control the presentation." According to him, every time his colleagues tried to restrict the program's possibilities and impose new frameworks, "they screwed up."

The inventor of PowerPoint is also particularly harsh about excessive and systematic use of the program. He calls for more simplicity and effort to make presentations readable. He suggests that images and all kinds of effects be limited, because fancy effects distract from the message. And above all he urges all PowerPoint users to "resist the lure of . . . flying bullet points."[34]

Gaskins observes that audiences rarely complain about too little embellishment but are easily offended by too much. More profoundly, with a kind of lucidity after the fact, Gaskins acknowledges that a polished presentation often requires a darkened room, so that "discussion and questions [are] discouraged," and that the aim of these presentations is often to "amaze the audience with technical and visual wizardry."

With Kodak's announcement in 2003 that it was halting production of slide projectors, the die was cast. The only remaining method for projecting slides was now a laptop computer, presentation software, and a video projector. Everyone could turn herself into a presentation designer and could mix all the techniques without worrying about coherence or need. Total improvisation ruled, and every presentation had to have animation, color, illustrations, and sound.

In Gaskins's view, these effects are of little use in a lecture or an argument. But the program makes all the effects so easy to produce that they have proliferated, and every presentation more and more tries to look like advertising.

> Despite the lush graphics effects so easily produced through modern presentation applications, most contemporary presentations should return to formats nearly as spare as the old overhead transparencies. It's not necessary to copy their specific limitations . . . but the equivalent level of disregard for extraneous decoration would be helpful, for the sake of both presenter focus and audience comprehension.

In short, he concludes, "the emphasis should be more matter with less art."[35]

2

ANOTHER WAY OF WORKING

➡

The appearance of PowerPoint at the dawn of the 1990s came at a key moment in the history of organizations. Whereas the company of the 1960s operated according to highly bureaucratic and hierarchical managerial models, in which the social division of labor and the sacrosanct distinction between planning and execution reigned supreme, the company of the 1990s seemed to have freed itself from those rigidities. It valued cooperation, creativity, innovation, and autonomy, but also efficiency, competitiveness, and performance.

The project-driven organization has become the basic paradigm of contemporary management. No more "silos,"[1] independent divisions, "states within the state," or departments turned in on themselves; the time has come for "horizontality," "collaboration," "innovation," and "quality" at every level. New managerial terms have made their appearance: "goal contract," "project committee," "professional competence," "operational excellence," "evaluation interview," "matrix management," and so on.

Meetings, once occasional and limited, have become a daily work practice in which employees exchange ideas, discuss, arbitrate, and decide. A tool designed to communicate and distribute information in a particular setting (the work meeting), PowerPoint has become in a few years the favorite medium for generations of employees, notably in the service sector. Often it is the only workplace tool in addition to e-mail and Excel spreadsheets.

This ubiquitous use of PowerPoint, which some call a form of addiction, has engendered unprecedented practices in the exchange of ideas, the provision of information, and ways of deciding and working together.

Is PowerPoint addiction an effect or a cause? The employee is supposed to become autonomous, mobile, creative, able both to work in a team and to "sell himself," to promote his skills and his personality, skills that will allow him to propose or get involved in projects. The employee of the project-driven company is always on a mission; he is adaptable and innovative. And "knowledge of computer programs, notably Excel and PowerPoint, is a plus," as employment ads often specify.[2]

ONCE UPON A TIME, THERE WAS A ROCK-AND-ROLL COMPANY

These were the 1960s, when battalions of typists sat at their machines all day under the threatening gaze of a department head who reported to a division vice president who made a weekly report to his division president, and so on. Orders streamed down through the multiple layers of a thoroughly military pyramid. This was hardly surprising at a time when the "personnel manager"—"human resources" lay in the future—was half the time a retired military man (at forty-five, one could still begin a new career).

Following technological developments, the nearly universal

Taylorism that developed after World War I had undergone important changes. Automation had taken over many production sectors. But the overall operation of companies, whether industrial or service companies, had hardly changed. Organizations were highly hierarchical, the division of labor institutionalized, dialogue and discussion banned, innovation and change infrequent, and careers uniform and relatively unchanging. Tasks were standardized.

The world of the company was schematically divided into three categories: those who produced, the laborers; those who invented and created, the engineers; and those who managed and piloted, the bosses. In general, the two latter categories tended to come together to form the elite of the organization, the cadres, bringing together "experts" and "managers." For the role of a cadre was that of both experts in specific areas and managers able to supervise sizable teams. The expert was the "transmission belt" between managers and laborers. The cadre member saw to the application of decisions taken at the top and sometimes could bring up questions from below. Such a person in a 1960s company was troubled by this position "between a rock and a hard place," where he had no power, no decision-making authority, and no autonomy. He had to execute and deliver the result expected by the management.

Due to the weight of hierarchy, the growing automation of tasks, and the bureaucratic and compartmentalized organization, the company of the 1960s was becoming stifling. However, the growing dominance of service employment, with an intensification of administrative functions accompanied by the increasingly important role of information processing, produced change.[3] Information technology has become the sinews of war for every sector producing goods and services.[4] These techniques of drafting, copying, calculating, and transmitting information—techniques whose history began in the nineteenth century—have substantially transformed ways of working.

With regard to organization, the 1960s were marked by the reign of triumphant rationalization, authority, the race for progress, and attachment to the sense of security of employment or professional status. In terms of management, these trends often took the form of conflict with authority, a split between creators and operators, standardization of operations, repetition of tasks, depersonalization, and lack of recognition and devaluation of individuals. In short, work was considered boring, monotonous, disempowering, and lacking in creativity.[5]

But impelled by various factors—competition, new managerial models, social conflict, falling profits, international constraints, and so on—companies had to change. Company managers realized that the lever of pay alone was no longer sufficient to motivate the troops; they had to give meaning to work and create real reasons to get involved.

Cadres had to be given career prospects other than advancement through seniority. The hierarchical and bureaucratic model was criticized and replaced by a type of organization in which participants were more autonomous, multi-specialists, participating in decision making. The Japanese Toyota model played a significant role, bringing to antiquated Taylorism the new charms of constant improvement, "just in time" delivery, and "zero delay." This was the time of the "lean, open, and stable company"[6]—"lean" because to be responsive, the company could no longer operate with multiple hierarchical ladders; "open" in the sense that organizations had to be streamlined and there should be no hesitation in relying on subcontractors; and "stable" because the organization had to be carefully planned.

In more general terms, companies sought to restore the individual to the center of things. The assembly-line worker was only a cog in a great machine or was the machine itself, but the modern company wanted to provide meaning, notably in the face of collective labor, and offer individuals the possibility of meeting their personal aspirations. Whereas the baby-boom years had instituted a break between individual and organization, the 1970s, experiencing the repercussions of the hunger for liberalization following 1968, witnessed new consideration for the individual in the personnel management of companies.

THE PROJECT MANAGEMENT COMPANY

According to the new management gurus, the 1980s represented the return of the individual in the company.[7] It operated as a network organized around small autonomous teams. It mobilized employees with a clear vision and pursued an ambitious goal, all guided by the charisma of its leaders. To be efficient and profitable, it outsourced operations that were not its core business, gathered experts around itself, and strove to respond to customer needs, all for the benefit of its shareholders alone.

For management manuals in the 1990s, work and companies were supposed to create the conditions for personal fulfillment by a proliferation of projects. In its managerial sense, a project is "a single process made up of a set of coordinated and controlled activities with start and end dates, undertaken with the purpose of achieving a goal that meets specific requirements."[8] In other words, a project is the coordinated action of diverse resources with a precise goal for a limited period of time.

This type of management first appeared in the 1950s in major areas of engineering, such as energy, transportation, and construction. In the face of increased demand and a constant reduction in time allowed, organizations that were vertically divided by function became more horizontal; the project mode made it possible to save time. This way of working transformed industrial organization and changed the roles, relations, tools, and interactions among various participants in the production process.

But the project is more than a means of management; it defines a paradigm that Luc Boltanski and Ève Chiapello identify in *The New Spirit of Capitalism*,[9] and that extends beyond the world of business: "A social structure by projects or a general organization of society by projects. The city by projects, for example, is presented as a system of constraints weighing on the networked world (a world that can be termed connectionist) impelling us to weave connections and extend their ramifications only while respecting the maxims of justifiable action appropriate to projects."[10]

In the twenty-first century, participants have every interest in playing their own game, to the degree that this no longer involves taking one's place in a comfortable linear career but rather entering into the effervescent mobility of projects. Thus the employee is no longer judged and used according to qualifications and the exercise of a particular profession but on the ability to change, adapt, be versatile. His supervisors will also evaluate commitment, relational skills, and qualities as a communicator: "Neo-management looks to what are increasingly called 'life skills,' as opposed to knowledge and *savoir faire*."[11] The company therefore encourages its employees to train themselves in the use of new tools, to be capable of constantly adapting themselves, to sell projects, and even to engage in self-promotion, to move from project to project in order to demonstrate their capacity for adaptation and their employability.

In the "projective city" identified by Boltanski and Chiapello, the governing principle is activity and the mode of relation is connection. The actions that characterize the projective city are:

connecting, communicating, coordinating, accommodating others, and trusting. To enjoy consideration in this city, one must be involved, flexible, versatile, autonomous, and so on. In these circumstances, supporters of the old school—authoritarian, rigid, anchored to their status, preferring security to movement—are condemned. The privileged instruments of the projective city are of course the new technologies, informal relations of trust, partnerships, alliances, subcontracting, networks, outsourcing, and autonomous units.

Can one imagine working today without a mobile phone or a laptop, without e-mail or the Internet? In an economic environment that lives at the instantaneous pace of financial markets and customer needs on a worldwide scale, companies have gradually given in to the "sort of injunction to communicate"[12] in every activity and in the minutest aspects of the organization of labor:

One can hardly work without communicating: work involves communication as much as technique. Almost all situations demonstrate that communication is necessary for the implementation of the intelligence of operators, the construction of a joint activity, the search for compromise. Nor can one organize work over the long term without organizing communication—through media, tools, rules, meetings, the arrangement of schedules, the design of appropriate spaces. And one cannot work in the long term without a collective social life, hence without opportunities to talk to one another.[13]

Communication has become a tool of production and execution necessary for the evaluation of work, planning, the transmission and circulation of instructions, discussion and negotiation, and the resolution of problems: "Communication is thus closely connected to operational methods, the management of knowledge, the organization of groups, the programming of work in time and space, the transmission of instructions, and the updating of rules and standards."[14] For twenty years, the multidisciplinary group Langage et Travail, bringing together sociologists, ergonomists, anthropologists, linguists, psychologists, and others, has been carefully following this evolution, not only of communication as such but of what the group defines as "the language share of work."

For his part, the sociologist Gérald Gaglio, who wrote a study of the use of PowerPoint in a marketing firm, summarizes this dynamic as follows:

> The growth of the "language share of work" has its source in the growth of the service sector of the economy, the advent of new information and communication technologies, and the development of "quality" procedures. More precisely, the use of digital slides is involved in two developments. First, as a participant in the "rise of written texts at work," this use derives from a rationalization of work through the written word [that goes back to] Taylorism. Gradually, the injunction to give an account of one's work reached all the hierarchical strata and presentations with digital slides are still contributing to it today. . . . Speaking up at work, in France particularly since the Auroux laws on participation in the 1980s, is given standing through the portmanteau word "communication." This injunction to communicate is reinforced by the "horizontality" desired and partially made possible by the adoption of organizational structures (matrixes) in fashion in recent years.[15]

Although the injunction to communicate extends beyond the framework of management by project, it is nonetheless one of its essential characteristics, notably through another one of management's favorite tools: the meeting.

"PROJECT" MEANS "MEETING"

The project mode, whose cardinal values are speed, constant exchange, reporting, the lowest cost, and continuous evaluation, has forced companies to make profound changes in their traditional means of communication (notes, memos, reports, and the like) and to develop new ones (e-mails, the Internet). Most important, it has transformed one of the central sites of the life of the company: the meeting.

Late-twentieth-century companies realized that meetings—particularly among peers—made it possible to resolve problems that could not be resolved by an isolated individual, even an expert. Meetings could do the job just as quickly with better results. The traditional meeting brought engineers together with engineers, all speaking the language of engineering, computer specialists with other computer specialists, and salesmen with other salesmen (maybe with someone from marketing thrown in). With the project company, the meeting was broadened, not only in its purposes (to inform, exchange, share, display, train, persuade, or mobilize), but also in its audience (team, department, sector, partner, subcontractor, supplier, customer, and so on). Meetings can now be regular and organized or informal and creative. Ubiquitous, the meeting has become one of the most common activities—and the most time-consuming, along with e-mail—in contemporary companies.

The meeting genre is rooted in standards originally established in a world based on paper, which have been transferred to the electronic media.[16] At a minimum, the meeting can be defined as an activity of communication organized around face-to-face exchanges, including a logistical element (time, place, physical arrangement, and so on), an agenda, an event/performance (the meeting itself), and a "deliverable"[17] (transcript, notes, reports, and so on). The way these modules are put together is left to the discretion of the organizers: logistics and agenda, for example, can overlap with an invitation containing both types of information. The agenda can be presented at the beginning of the meeting or distributed in advance. Finally a transcript may or may not exist, in various forms.

Meetings may be necessary on multiple occasions on various themes and for different audiences. They can be divided into three major families, depending on their purpose:

- *Work meetings*: budgetary, planning, organization, job, brainstorming, technical discussion, presentation of a process, or project reporting (management committee or project committee communication of the status of a project or program to evaluate the level of resources allocated, timing, and so on).
- *Information meetings* (lectures/training): management, executive, or department, calls for bids, reports, focus groups, and consumer meetings.
- *Communication meetings* (events, performances, shows): presentation of results or new products, sermons, convention rallies, lectures, seminars, colloquia, and so on.

In the category of work meetings, the meeting of a department, of management, or of a sector is one of the invariant events in any organization. It is an opportunity to provide an update on the department's activity, to solicit opinions, to speak of coming actions and problems encountered. Depending on the manager, the sector, and the audience, these meetings can be participatory or directed.

Project meetings, particularly involving computer services, take place in a context where all tools are much more standardized and formalized: the project committee is one of the essential tools of new management. At very regular intervals, various bodies involved in the project—generally divided between project management (the sector that needs a product, a service, or an application to carry out its business) and work supervisors (who must respond to the need, create the product, the service, or the application)—meet and exchange views using a paper medium.

These meetings make it possible to determine how far the project has advanced, to negotiate some points of disagreement, to bring dysfunctions into the open, and to make decisions, if appropriate. According to the manager of a Web project: "Mostly it's an opportunity to complain about unmet deadlines, cost overruns, or long unresolved problems. Presentations are usually validated by e-mail after the meeting and function as reference documents for the project." Above the project committee, a management committee—essentially made up of a hierarchy of superiors of each sector involved—meets more episodically to be informed, to arbitrate, and to make decisions that have often already been ratified lower down. This type of committee fits the model of the information meeting.

Information meetings generally require careful arrangements and visual presentation. A typical example is the recommendation from internal colleagues or, more often, from external service providers. This involves an agency, a consultant, a supplier, or another service presenting and selling a product, service, procedure, or the like. Not just a means of providing information and engaging in an exchange of ideas, the meeting becomes an exercise in persuasion and charm requiring a set of artifices that can sway a decision. The various techniques of presentation have been expanded by major consulting firms, advertising agencies, and marketing professionals (see chapter 7). In advertising, for example, meetings presenting recommendations for advertising campaigns usually use PowerPoint. Although their ultimate target is the customer, these presentations are generally conducted internally throughout development, so the campaign may be amended, commented on, changed, validated, and so on. The multiplicity of both internal and external participants requires the use of common communications media that enable sharing and exchange.

"MEETING" MEANS "PRESENTATION"

In barely twenty years, the meeting, which had not involved much in the way of communication, has evolved considerably. Today it is impossible to contemplate even a small meeting without presentation devices. A large number of managers and apprentice managers have even taken training courses or consulted the many manuals available in bookstores[18] that describe the rules and standards for running a successful meeting.

PowerPoint has become the indispensable medium for this kind of event. The software makes it possible to go quickly and to produce at low cost a simple, readable presentation accessible to everyone in a shared manner. It is an efficient, productive, attractive tool that has a worldwide "evangelical" character. Above all, PowerPoint is a universal language that makes it possible to promote the virtues of the new management: the ability to synthesize, simplification, an aptitude for visualization, an inclination toward collegiality, collaborative work, and horizontality. The software makes it possible to technify and automate the means of production of ideas and institutes a new kind of circulation of activities, relations, and exchanges in the workplace. In short, PowerPoint contains the qualities demanded of the neo-managers of the twenty-first-century company.

The three types of meeting defined above correspond to three uses of the software that Robert Gaskins planned for, according to the audience and the quality required for presentations. The minimal level of polish, basic PowerPoint, is advised for internal work meetings. The superior level, requiring color slides and a higher quality level, is recommended for more formal meetings with more important customers or audiences; this type of presentation requires more time and resources. And the multimedia level, very spectacular, is advised for more theatrical occasions when the primary goal is to distract a large audience.

Gérald Gaglio proposes another division of presentations into three types according to their purpose and content: a "technical discussion" type, designed to inform the audience about something new; a "sharing knowledge" type, in which the speaker presents his group and its activity to another group in the hope of setting up a collaboration; and a "study or programs or projects" type, designed to communicate the status of a project or a program and to evaluate the state of the resources allocated.[19]

In the 1960s and 1970s, presentations were designed by upper management, written down, and often communicated with solemnity. Frédéric R. recalls his years of running commercial meetings: "Even in the 1980s, a director or manager would write his speech and afterward on the basis of this text one could create transparencies to illustrate the different points of the speech, with graphs or illustrations. At the time, a good deal of effort was put into the underlying argument and the organization of the speech. And then, one turned to the graphic form."

Organizations have many "genres"[20] of communication—

notes, letters, e-mails, forms, reports, and so on. Socially accepted as means of communication and permanently adopted by
the members of the organization, these genres adopt normalized
and institutional models that shape all communications activity
among collaborators in a given environment. As soon as Power-
Point presentations began to dominate in small meetings as well
as larger gatherings, all presentations imperceptibly morphed
into commercial demonstrations: to be effective, one had to focus
on the essential, display the strong points, bring forward the key
concepts, promote action, and so on. The idea of collective work,
with thinking based on debate and the exchange of views, became
difficult because it was less efficient, not fast enough, therefore
not profitable, and in the end old-fashioned. PowerPoint definitively transformed the work meeting into a spectacle.

AN ARTISTIC AND PARTICIPATIVE EMPLOYEE

The PowerPoint means of communication favors the development of a certain form of discourse in the company. This mode
is so dominant that it requires participants to master both the
skills and the behavior necessary for its use to be able to stay in
the organization.

The company of the 1990s valued the "multiexpert," able to
work with everyone and to adapt to all situations, a person who
did not hang on to status or privileges but liked to change and
move in a project in which a team is committed as a group with a
shared interest in satisfying the client, internal or external. This
constraint became both a mobilizing element and the criterion
for evaluating any activity.

To increase productivity, make working conditions attractive,
improve quality, and increase profits, the necessary and sought-
after skills, at least in theory, are autonomy, spontaneity, mobil-

ity, teamwork, multicompetence and multiactivity (as opposed to specialization and the logic of a profession), conviviality, availability, creativity, and openness to others. Importance is given to personal experience rather than qualifications and knowledge. The new employee "knows also how to *give of himself*, to be there as and when appropriate, to exploit his *presence* in personal relations, in face-to-face encounters: he is always available, even-tempered, self-assured without being arrogant, familiar without overstepping the limits, obliging, with more to offer than he expects in return."[21]

It is indispensable to know how to present oneself to facilitate exchanges while demonstrating one's flexibility, in order never to place oneself in a position of authority. The employee of the twenty-first century does not claim an expertise or a position; she can direct or allow herself to be directed.

The PowerPoint presentation in many cases turns out to be the ideal medium for a kind of collective creation in which each participant is expected to contribute. It amounts to co-authorship of a publicly formulated document:[22] the slide becomes an expressive element that everyone can help create, change, imitate, transmit, and so on. This collective drafting represents an extension of the function of writing that corresponds to the contemporary demand for generalized expressivity.

It is hardly surprising that the first major users of PowerPoint often came from sectors ruled by collective creativity, such as advertising. According to François L., a young advertising man, "There is something euphoric in collective creation, jubilation in a rush job. Often three or four of us will stay at the agency late into the night to prepare our presentation, finding original devices that will get us the budget. It's pretty intoxicating. Anyhow, it's better than sitting alone in front of your computer drawing little graphs."

The advantage of PowerPoint also lies in the fact that the result is immediately visible and can be instantaneously modified. For a financier, an engineer, a trainer, it is very stimulating to be able to manipulate, draft, or modify in real time. More and more consultants prepare their slides on the spot in work meetings.

PowerPoint made it possible to "democratize" the preparation of graphic presentations, to make their creation accessible to everyone. Departments often have specialists who know how to work quickly and well, but everyone can be taught to make slides. Although the software encourages collective creation and teamwork, it can also paradoxically emancipate some employees from supervision. And there are indeed many amateurs who love to make their own presentations, sure of their esthetic sense, which can finally be expressed in the workplace. Everyone can compose his own work free of constraint. According to André D., a French designer in the United States, "Thanks to the software, a large number of engineers, managers, and financiers turn themselves into creative workers from one day to the next by devoting hours and hours to concocting beautiful presentations rather than to their basic job. What is serious is that they lose interest in everything but the form, they produce graphically incoherent slides, and they completely forget to work on their message." We will see later that this deviation is not the result of chance or of bad habits but is inherent in the PowerPoint software.

At a time when, as Andy Warhol put it, "In the future everyone will be world-famous for 15 minutes," when putting one's personal profile on Facebook or professional profile on LinkedIn takes the place of a vehement affirmation of one's identity, when the scenes of ordinary life become the primary elements in TV scripts or song lyrics, and when it is essential to show to the largest audience one's life and works, the handling of a tool like PowerPoint perfectly satisfies the injunction to stage oneself as part of the culture of narcissism that appeared at the end of the thirty years of postwar prosperity.[23] It enables one to demonstrate one's creative talent, one's ability to present an argument, give it form, and interpret it; it enables one to justify one's existence, to prove one's aptitude to do a job, and to remain useful to the organization.

This exhibition of oneself is designed to sell oneself, to shine in front of others, to make one's performance visible, to advertise oneself: "The logic of the company requires the presence of this kind of software, which lends itself to use even before the production of any real content by making it possible essentially to present competencies and exhibit a methodology. In this economic and organizational framework, PowerPoint becomes a tool for selling a project."[24]

So it is not any elements of content that might convince, but the staging of the expertise as a kind of playlet in which the actors' performance, appropriate use of props, and the overall presentation are often more decisive than the answers to the questions raised. According to Marc A., a public relations consultant, "It is true that in presentations of bids, particularly in the area of public relations, it is often the staging and the quality of the medium that wins the day, particularly on jobs with fixed costs and time limits." In addition, the linear, sequential, and univocal character of the presentation, a form that makes the presentation very close to a slide show or a documentary film, accentuates the dramatic effects and instills an emotional element into a world of reason.

"TIME IS MONEY"

It is now a commonplace that time constraint is a key element in the success of any project.[25] For participants in the project as well as for the final client, meeting deadlines is *the* essential factor of success. For the majority of company participants, the use of a tool like PowerPoint represents at first sight an incomparable time-saver. According to Cécile L., manager in a public relations consulting firm, "Our clients are more and more demanding about deadlines: they ask us systematically to do yesterday what's due tomorrow. With PowerPoint we can work quickly, summarily, and effectively. If you're not too literary, like me, you cut to the chase right away: two ideas, three objectives, five actions and everything is wrapped up. It may be mediocre at bottom, but it's often enough to win the job. You have to organize your presentation well, supplement and illustrate your speech, and be committed."

Time constraints are such that sometimes companies are forced to subcontract their presentations. Some European consulting firms have managed to save time by taking advantage of time zones, having their slides made at night in the United States: ordered in the evening, they're delivered the next morning (see chapter 6).

The constant reduction of time allowed also rather mechanically imposes the fusion of the documents presented, the deliverables, combining those designed for the presentation (the slides) and those submitted for reading, reporting, and study. A medium for oral presentation, PowerPoint has become increasingly the only deliverable. Slides are simultaneously a visual aid to support the oral exposé and the only official written document for an operation—the report summarizing the results and the conclusions of a project or a job. The sociologist Valérie Baudouin observes:

> Subject to an intensification of the pace of work, the producer has to optimize the time of development of "deliverables."

Making transparencies requires less time than drafting a report. Previous presentations can easily be reused, because they are a set of disjointed texts that can be recombined and rearranged at lower cost. The transparency file also has a major asset: it makes possible real saving in production by functioning as a presentation medium and a report (two for one). Not to mention the fact that an "injunction" has developed to make presentations with transparencies. Isn't the success of a presentation with transparencies generally tied to the search by organizations for maximum responsiveness and optimal utilization of a precious resource, time?[26]

Created with this dual purpose, slides do not, however, meet either the requirements of an oral exposé or those of a written report. As we shall see, they have too much text to be effective visual aids (to support, not eclipse, the speaker), but too few elements to meet the obligations of a report or a study. But practitioners themselves recognize the economic value of "killing two birds with one stone," even if an adaptation is necessary to rearrange the slides on paper. More and more consultants have been sprucing up their presentations along these lines to make documents that become very carefully prepared presentation tablets.

Systematic copying or recycling is another method of gaining time. PowerPoint presentations were in fact the first victims of the endemic computer illness: cut and paste.

Who hasn't witnessed a presentation dealing with one establishment with a signature at the bottom of the page mentioning another organization? Consultants are inclined to think it futile to develop original presentations for identical or similar problems. To fulfill criteria of efficiency and speed, they have no scruples about reproducing, with adjustments, presentations designed for another client in the same sector for the same service.

Recycling has become so commonplace that some firms have databases that group presentations according to different types of projects, called "frameworks." Anyone can thus put together a collection of presentations and preferred templates and create very attractive presentations with little creative effort by relying exclusively on the work of others. This is all the more true because this reproduction of models has acquired a sort of legitimacy of representation that lends seriousness to the document.

A MEDIUM OF CONTROL

In the process of construction, to the extent that a presentation is generally carefully reviewed and validated a large number of times, it acquires a degree of conformity and even legitimacy. The final display of the presentation, whatever the context, presupposes a form of sovereignty, authority, or reputation. For presenting always means exposing oneself to the gaze and the judgment of others. Behind the presentation always lies the desire to transmit an objective, a result, or the status of an activity, research project, job, operation, project, product, or service.

In organizations, presentations sanction and make possible validation and control by one's peers. PowerPoint can function as evidence, a justification of the task accomplished. Finally, it presents itself as a medium that guarantees through its very controlled status an a priori legitimacy offering reassurance for any decision that might be made.

According to Boltanski and Chiapello, the question of control was a major preoccupation of the management theorists of the 1990s:

One of their main problems is controlling a "liberated firm" (to use Tom Peters's expression) composed of self-organized teams working in a network that is not unified in time or space. "Controlling the uncontrollable" is not something with an infinite number of solutions: in fact, the only solution is for people to *control themselves*, which involves transferring constraints from external organizational mechanisms to people's internal dispositions.[27]

This amounts to a kind of double bind,[28] which consists of promoting the creativity of agents while transforming this laudable demand into an obligation or even a means of control. This reversal is especially perverse because it focuses not on the roles and functions of the individual in the organization, but on his personal, inner, psychological resources, his capacity to express himself.[29] In the guise of liberating speech, the organization subjects its employees to a form of self-control with effects that are far more pernicious than old-fashioned reprimands because they affect self-confidence and emotion more than reflection and reason.

This manner that companies have adopted of praising the autonomy of individuals is intended to make them take charge themselves of the control previously exercised by the hierarchy. Everyone becomes the supervisee and the supervisor of the others. Boltanski and Chiapello even show how the general focus of every company and every administration on the satisfaction of the customer represents only a variant of this new form of control, so that anyone who does not adopt the customer focus is considered inefficient and must be expelled from the community.

Thus a formal role is assigned to the presentation. The product serves as evidence of the work of exchanges and procedures that has been accomplished. The presentation demonstrates the activity, especially because in most cases it will be used as a deliverable for clients, participants, decision makers, colleagues, and students.

PowerPoint appears to be a visually inoffensive but extremely powerful weapon of this culture of control, reporting, auditing. It displays all the tools needed to evaluate individuals for their ability to organize a speech, meet objectives, communicate, work in a team, and so on. The culture of the presentation implicitly describes the ideal employee of the early twenty-first century: an autonomous and creative "collaborator" who likes to work in a team and knows how to communicate but is constantly subject to the gaze and the judgment of others in the context of meetings and presentations that operate as so many trial scenes and sites for evaluation.

3

BULLET-POINT RHETORIC

➡

PowerPoint is a medium of its time: conceived at the dawn of the automated office, the software "exploded" when office organization experienced deep changes. This change can be seen in the very way in which PowerPoint presentations are constructed, in their discursive and graphic structures, and in their modes of exposition.

From their very first appearance in the late 1980s, the bulk of PowerPoint presentations consisted of lists of words augmented with bullet points and vaguely illustrated with graphs, tables, and even some photographs, in a landscape format, that is, a horizontal A4 or letter-size page matching the screen format. In the 2000s, a reading of numerous presentations in many areas shows that the text, even in very simplified form, still accounts for 80 to 90 percent of the content of slides in every presentation.

But in the most common PowerPoint manuals,[1] the strictly textual aspect of the presentation never seems to be an issue: discourse, words, syntax, and lexicon are discussed little or not at all. Authors of these guides are more interested in problems of graphic format: choice of typography, hierarchy of reading, interline spacing, direction of arrows, form of tables, and the like, or the more general organization of the slide show.

In short, these manuals teach technical mastery of the tool and graphic arrangement: how to create one's first presentation, how to integrate graphs or photographs, how to publish on the Internet. They neglect all discursive aspects: how to organize one's speech, how to title, how to construct an argument that makes sense. Not a line, or almost none, on the writing. The authors probably assume, as people do in the world of business, that everyone knows how to write and organize ideas.

A NARROWED RANGE OF LANGUAGE: POWERPOINT SYNTAX

This pedagogical void in the area of composition, this negligence with regard to discourse, has a simple explanation: the PowerPoint format favors a mode of communication in which words seem emptied of any substance. Merely consulting several presentations in the area of economics and finance, the kind organized for shareholders' meetings or for the presentation of the annual earnings report, is enough to take the measure of this linguistic impoverishment.

The first element read on a slide is the title. Beginning with the headline, the syntax is rigid and the lexicon impoverished. Formulations are repetitive, wording elliptical, and expressions catchalls: An Organization in Marching Order, Sustained Growth, Significant Improvement, A Strained Environment, Fierce Competition, A Volatile Market, Solid Fundamentals, An Atypical Context, Impacted Level of Activity, and so on. By the use of ready-made formulations and empty words, discourse shrinks and becomes merely a site for the commonplaces of media and economic Newspeak.

David Farkas, an American professor of design who has taken a serious interest in PowerPoint, brings out three of the primary constraints connected with the writing of slides, particularly titles, that give rise to this contraction of meaning. First he shows how the constraint of the format encourages designers to reduce their titles to the minimum ("content cutting"), so that they often become incomprehensible or dull. He then points to the tendency to have a message or title pass from one slide to another ("overflow distortion"), often with an ellipsis, thus: Establishment of the Fourth European Participant in the Management of Assets . . . , then on the next slide, . . . Through the Merger of the Asset Management Departments of Two Major Groups.[2] Finally and most important, he notes the semantic poverty of the titles ("slide title flattening"), because the format and largely institutional use encourages designers to avoid titles that are too evocative or meaningful.[3]

The vocabulary used for these titles—as for the bulk of presentations—is reduced to a few dozen words taken from economic and financial Newspeak, using and abusing euphemism, lexical shrinkage, ellipsis, and even "semantic wringing out."

This Newspeak is characterized by a few semantic obsessions, such as the immoderate use of the military and even the ballistics lexicon. There is constant talk of tactics, strategy, (re)conquest, campaign, position, impact, general mobilization, target, road map, launch window, security, and so on. The purpose of this martial lexicon is to show—to an audience that might not yet know it or has forgotten it—that economic competition is harsh and requires the mobilization of the most warlike resources, even in language, to motivate the troops and convince the shareholders.[4]

But we should also mention the use of Anglicisms, inappropriate Frenchifying, the arsenal of "globish,"[5] and the abuse of acronyms and abbreviations that often makes slides completely enigmatic. These are the shortcuts, reflexes, and simplifications that enable the designer of a PowerPoint presentation, because of the constraints of speed and efficiency, to relieve herself of the burden of thinking necessary for the proper development of an argument. Why do something complicated when you can do something simple, especially if the tool at hand favors precisely the elementary?

But if PowerPoint encourages Newspeak, it also has its own constraints and its particular grammar.

Among these procedures is nominalization, which consists of changing a sentence (with a verb)—the most common construction—into a noun phrase. Inspired by the language of advertising and Anglo-American headlines, this artifice makes it possible to shorten an utterance, transforming it into a formula or a slogan. It appeared in the written press in France in the 1980s under the influence of papers like *Libération* and *Actuel.*

This type of metamorphosis changes a subject and verb into a noun and adjective, making it possible to "condense in a single utterance what would have taken two utterances in succession."[6] For example, under the constraint of summarizing, nominalization has become one of the primary characteristics of PowerPoint writing. It takes different forms depending on whether it is a verb or an adjective that is being changed into a noun (The Volatility of the Markets, The Rationalization of Production) or whether the operation is carried out through semantic association (These Choices Dominated becomes The Prevalence of These Choices).

The first effect of the procedure is to artificially neutralize the utterance, along the lines of a scientific formula. "The shift of the phrase to a noun group erases the signs of person, tense, and aspect."[7] Nominalization has a perceptible effect on "information [that] is not distributed identically in a sentence and in a noun group . . . the informational role of a noun group derived from nominalization is different according to its position in the sentence (subject or object). Finally, nominalization carries assumptions that do not exist if one replaces the group by the corresponding sentence." There is in fact a semantic slippage making it possible both to provide a neutralized and decontextualized formulation and to foreground an element of the sentence that would not have been as visible in a traditional utterance. For example, such titles as Revival of Activity, Growth of the Combined Ratio, Slowdown of the Market, and so on place more emphasis on the quality—revival, growth—than on the theme itself: the attribute takes precedence over the subject. This procedure provides a "positive" commentary, while at the same time assuming a posture of impartiality, objectivity, and distance.

If this technique is used systematically in virtually every presentation, it is also because of the Anglo-American origin of the techniques of presentation. The influence of English, the international language of business, and of its structure, gives rise to forms of telegraphic writing in which nominalization occupies a large space. A language of universal communication, the English language thus imposes its constraints and a specific mode of linguistic construction. The omission of some connecting words; the modification of word order, notably the inversion of nouns and adjectives; and morphological changes to some words, notably words with the suffix -isation that have become relatively common in French, all demonstrate that this Anglo-American contamination is nothing new.[8] But new technologies, financial globalization, and their various media of communication have amplified the process of Anglicization and hence a certain standardization of local languages.

PowerPoint thereby tends to transform every *living* language into an institutional, bureaucratic, administrative idiom in which ready-made formulas and all-purpose expressions flourish.

The use of the indefinite article is an evocative example. In many presentations there is an accumulation of lapidary utterances such as "*a* rapid growth," "*a* noticeable rise," "*a* volatile market," and so on. Strengthening the force of the word, the "indefinite" term takes on a particular value.[9] In our example, "*the* market is volatile" would be vague, ordinary, and not very vivid. "*A* volatile market" has a more abrupt tone, which also emphasizes the adjective. The interest of this kind of designation is its indistinct character that can be interpreted in a specific or a generic way. This way of using the indefinite article makes it possible to join, in a sense, the particular and the universal and to make language neutral and distant. It gives the presentation a legitimate form acceptable to the largest possible audience.

Maintaining a facade of neutrality, the language of PowerPoint also has the power to command, through the excessive use of verbs in the infinitive: rationalize, promote, favor, sensitize, capitalize, construct, secure, ensure, develop, deploy, and so on.* The list of verbs returning imperturbably in every presentation could be extended indefinitely.

The infinitive defines the verb in the dictionary; it is the most neutral form. Although it has multiple uses in written language, the use that interests us here, the "institutional" infinitive, is what grammarians prefer to call the jussive or imperative infinitive:

---

* The examples, given in French infinitive form, correspond to the English infinitive without *to*; the purposes of this usage are explained in the next paragraph (translator).

An infinitive, even if used alone with no object, can say as much as a whole sentence. It then tends to take on the value of a command. . . . The infinitive has something colder, less amiable, more strictly technical than the imperative; it merely gives the direction to be followed with no expression of feeling. It is by definition impersonal (unaffected by the grammatical category of the person). With the infinitive, the command seems to emanate from no one and to be addressed to no one in particular.[10]

Every PowerPoint document thus seems to have no status, no audience, no author. According to an official who criticizes the depersonalized character of these documents: "There is a kind of dilution of responsibility that makes it possible not to question too much the sequence of the arguments, because the document has no specific status: it is neither a note, a report, nor a tool to help in decision making." This removal of responsibility or decontextualization disembodies the document, makes it immaterial, and endows it with a relative legitimacy, indeed a sovereignty, connected to this appearance of universality and often flimsiness.

For example, phrases like "capitalize on our model," "ensure a strong growth," "develop our offer," "strengthen our actions of optimization," or "grow faster than the market" all represent "positive" and "mobilizing" objectives. Vague and voluntarist slogans, these messages are theoretically designed to galvanize the group and set it on the right "win-win" path.[11] This assertive power of the infinitive is reinforced by the use of verbs of action to place every proposition within the idea of movement and the dynamic: mobilize, develop, accelerate, intensify, improve, optimize, reinforce, conquer, and so on. With no precise content, practically routine, these formulas have primarily a performative use, like commands from a sports coach. This is hardly surprising when one considers that a large number of presentations function like celebrations to unite and glorify the company: everyone must be convinced of the validity of the choices made by the management, on the basis of very general messages that could be applied to any company at all. PowerPoint makes precisely that possible without too much involvement or too much effort.

It is here that one of the many paradoxes of PowerPoint is located: although the presentation is an activity often constructed like a personal performance with staging and dynamic gadgets, one witnesses a "freezing" of language. More deeply, the rhetorical apparatus of the PowerPoint meeting produces an effect of depersonalization and the absence of individual responsibility. It is, in short, a perverse arrangement that gives pride of place to the speaker, to the power of his performance, while erasing his words and the definite meaning of his discourse and prescriptions: a subtle association between the power of evocation held by a speaker in the posture of a preacher relying on a thoroughly institutionalized and normalized discourse that comes close to recalling certain communications setups in various totalitarian regimes.

THE BULLET-POINT OBSESSION

The foundation and heart of PowerPoint language is the bullet point. The name of the software, of course, explicitly refers to the power of those little points.[12] With PowerPoint, the reign of the list as privileged mode of communication arrived. All kinds of lists: simple, alphabetical, hierarchical, graduated, disseminated, illustrated, animated, linear, and vertical for agendas, summaries, actions, objectives, results, and so on.

PowerPoint did not invent the list, the use of which can be

detected at the very beginnings of writing. In a pathbreaking study of the relationship between oral and written expression, the American anthropologist Jack Goody notes that "the making of tables, lists, and formulae" is characteristic of the earliest forms of writing.[13] The invention of writing made it possible to provide a concrete, permanent, and "objective" medium for speech. This form of neutrality provided to language by writing is, however, a two-edged sword. At the outset, writing had two primary functions: preserving speech and shifting from the oral to the visual. The great interest of writing was its combinatorial aspect: words became autonomous units that could be shifted, extracted, changed, transposed, and so forth. But writing also decontextualized the word from the act of enunciation. If in time it acquired a form of authority compared to speech, this was because it depersonalized discourse, erased the origin of the utterance, and thereby profoundly changed all cognitive processes connected with language.

The earliest known written texts—in cuneiform in Mesopotamia in the third millennium B.C.—have nothing to do with the spoken word. They are basically economic, administrative, or legal texts—business documents—and "the most characteristic form is something that rarely occurs in oral discourse at all (though it sometimes appears in ritual), namely, the list."[14]

Presenting a text in the form of a list results in a basic difference from the oral mode (and the usual written mode): it creates discontinuity. Goody deduces from this that the fact of using lists ought to have had an influence on the way transactions were conducted and also on the corresponding modes of thought. A list has a beginning, an end, a meaning, a direction; it can be read in different directions: from top to bottom, from right to left; it is easily organized by numbering, by initials, or by categories. It is closer to a picture or a formula than to the spoken word. The list has a separating, reductive, simplifying effect. Lists make information more visible and readable but also more abstract, and "they stand opposed to the continuity, the flux, the connectedness of the usual speech forms, that is, conversation, oratory, etc., and substitute an arrangement in which concepts, verbal items, are separated not only from the wider context in which speech always, or almost always, takes place, but separated too from one another, as in the inventory of an estate."[15]

In these simple, ordered lists, information is thus removed from its context in terms both of the social situation and of the linguistic realm. They seem to aspire to neutrality, the absence of discursive qualification, moving from the qualitative to the quantitative (counting rather than description, enumeration rather than characterization, accumulation rather than meaning, inventory rather than valuation). Providing visual or graphic material that is easily modified, plastic, and flexible, the list is then reusable, generalizable, and customizable. In other words, it manufactures standards.

"The arrangement of words (or 'things') in a list is itself a mode of classifying, of defining a 'semantic field,' since it includes some and excludes others. Moreover it places those items in a hierarchy."[16] This way of organizing data creates forms of meaning, intended or not. By enumerating, listing, cataloging, one classifies, hierarchizes, organizes the world. In short, making a list means proposing a certain view of the world. And using the list as a primary language means (giving the illusion of) speaking the language of order and mastery.

According to Jack Goody, this arrangement of knowledge made possible the development of scientific discourse, that is, logical thinking succeeding "savage thought."[17] A certain system of abstraction (*mathesis*), of rational objectivity, has replaced a subjectivity that is never controlled or channeled.

A tool that makes lists gives its users the highest guarantee of rationality, rock-solid legitimacy. PowerPoint imitates a model of scientific organization, control, and patterning that fits perfectly in the world of business, where the tyranny of expertise and (pseudo-)objectivity reigns.

But the story becomes troubling when one recognizes that the generalization of bullet points paradoxically destroys an element that ought to be at the heart of every presentation: logical sequencing and a smooth argument. In a 2003 article widely circulated on the Web and devoted to Microsoft tools, a pioneer of the new economy, Rafi Haladjian, denounced the illusion of describing the world by means of lists: "instead of arguing, you only have to stack up, count, 'bullet-list,' and string out verbs in the infinitive." The effects are obvious: they give the "illusion of a perfect mastery of the world" and tell a story running in a single direction following an unchangeable thread.[18]

How can one not admire, for example, the way this company can recount the development of its primary sectors of activity in a few bullet points:

- Decline in leather goods on high comparative bases
- Slowing of activity in ready-to-wear
- Continuation of sustained growth in footwear
- Good performance of beauty royalties

One can go very far in this register of bullet-point narrative, as indicated by this slide from a presentation titled "The Death of Jesus Christ":

Jesus Is Crucified

- Jesus is brought before the court.
- The soldiers clothe him in purple.

- They crown him with thorns.
- They put a reed in his hand.
- They kneel mockingly before him.
  - "And began to salute him, Hail, King of the Jews!" Mark 15:18.
- They spit upon him.
- They strike him on the head with the reed.[19]

Edward Tufte has showed that the format imposed by the program makes it impossible to express relationships between the various themes or points set out. "For the naïve, bullet lists may create the appearance of hard-headed organized thought. But in the reality of day-to-day practice, the PP cognitive style is faux-analytical, with a bias towards promoting effects without causes."[20] When the content of each slide is a series of detailed plans, it is indeed difficult to determine the connections between the different points. For example, if one has three points, A, B, C, should they be interpreted as completely disjointed elements, as a succession of elements (A then B then C), as elements connected by a causal link (A therefore B therefore C), or as some combination of these three relationships? To be sure, the oral performance generally makes it possible to clarify the logical connections among the elements of the demonstration. But what happens when the audience gets the document, the deliverable, and has to reconstruct the argument?

The list format restricts the capacity for continuous thought and makes it difficult for a fluid argument to emerge. By misrepresenting relationships and articulations between the elements in a chain, the list facilitates a form of argumentative mystification: a changed and manipulative relationship between cause and effect. Through its ability to compare lists of items, to set heterogeneous pieces of information end to end, PowerPoint fosters wrongful correlations: for example, the age of sellers and the penetration of a given product. Juxtaposition does not establish a causal relationship. But that relationship is insinuated, provoked by textual and visual proximity. One could cite multiple correlations that are just as fanciful as, for example, the relationship between increased sales of transistors and the number of inmates in psychiatric hospitals, demonstrating that transistors drive people crazy. One could also, by juxtaposing two lists or three curves, demonstrate that the profits of a firm's subsidiaries are inversely proportional to the age or educational level of its managers. According to Vincent T., former consultant in a major firm, now independent: "You have to realize that 90 percent of consultants' analyses consist of demonstrating correlations without proving the slightest cause and effect relationship between the phenomena described."

Very concrete demonstrations of the harmful effects of the use of bullet lists can often be found in the best business journals, such as the prestigious *Harvard Business Review*. And who is in a better position than representatives of 3M, the company that invented the transparency for overhead projectors, to become "prosecutors" of the bullet point, even though they helped propagate its use around the world?

In an article published in 1998, Gordon Shaw, executive director of planning and international at 3M, and his two co-authors noted their own inability to present strategic plans in a narrative form that would persuade an audience, even though 3M was a company that loved to tell stories about its business and its products (particularly how they were invented). "It's remarkable that we abandon storytelling when we do our strategic planning," they lamented.[21]

What did they use at 3M to formulate plans? As in all companies, lists, titles, and bullets. The authors choose three rather generic items as examples:

- Increase market share by 25%.
- Increase profits by 30%.
- Increase new-product introductions to ten a year.

This form of expression provides no picture, no idea of the organization, the market, or the customers. It is impossible to deduce them from this list, which does not say how these goals are connected to one another. More seriously, several radically different strategies could be represented by these three points; hence the risks of misinterpretation created by the visible lack of logical connections: will improving marketing increase market share, and will growing profits make possible investments for the development of new products? Or will the development of new products result from the combination of increased market share and higher profits? Or will profits make it possible to increase market share through advertising and the development of new products? And so on. All options are open.

The authors' point is simple: lists are valuable because they reduce complex situations to simple points; they make it possible to give the presenter relative autonomy; they reduce the speaker's stress in a high-stakes presentation, because he can rely on a document that seems clean and simple even though it deals with complex and troubling subjects. But as the authors point out, "writing is thinking," not simply arranging bullet points enabling you to "skip the stage of thinking," while giving the illusion that you are constructing a carefully thought-out plan when you are merely listing certain desirable actions to perform.

The conclusion is clear: the use of the list form reveals a "certain intellectual laziness."

Aside from the lack of logical connections, a list is too general and applies to all kinds of activities; it never emphasizes the specifics of an activity, an organization, or a market. Gordon Shaw also notes that the strategic plans presented at 3M never reflect the thinking, the vision, the idea of the company, its values, its culture, and that they never inspire enthusiasm.

These recurrent lists of items that are found in every institutional presentation, whether at IBM, Total, Halliburton, Merck, or Toyota—Reduce costs, Simplify processes, Accelerate growth—are "verbal images," standardized ritual formulas providing cold messages designed to neutralize the attention of the audience: shareholders, analysts, journalists, or employees who will in fact retain only a few numbers and two or three vague messages.

This bullet-pointing of language produces a cognitive framework that also imposes graphic hierarchies. The technique of sections, subsections, and so on, implies a single, closed direction, often decreasing (from top to bottom), and it forces the spectator to favor the higher point and disregard the lower point. Discourse and reasoning are reduced to a kind of flow chart in which one favors certain points made more readable, along the lines of Windows Explorer and its menu tree logic.

This structure confirms a famous law of new technologies, Conway's law. For Melvin Conway, a computer scientist who formulated it in 1968, organizations that design systems, particularly computer systems, are constrained to produce designs that copy the communication structures of these organizations. One can argue that most Microsoft products therefore diffuse their own cognitive frameworks. Many software programs designed by Microsoft operate by relying on the notion of the tree menu that is the trademark of Windows. Developing a presentation with PowerPoint generally consists of setting out lists like so many lines of computer programming with indentation, bullet points, and ever smaller type.

Edward Tufte emphasizes this point in his detailed analysis of a series of 2003 NASA slides about the *Columbia* space shuttle. On February 1, 2003, the shuttle broke up during atmospheric reentry, killing the seven crew members. According to the investigation conducted after the accident, eighty-two seconds after launch a piece of foam insulation weighing 760 grams broke loose and caused damage that led to the disintegration of the shuttle twelve days later. Engineers had detected the same type of problem many times before and had informed NASA. But mission control had decided that the evidence showing this kind of impact to be a danger was unconvincing. All reports had been prepared using PowerPoint.

In his demonstration, Tufte focuses particularly on one slide out of a series of twenty-eight that were later presented to an investigating board. He points to a "festival of bureaucratic hyper-rationalism," with six different levels of text to arrange and classify eleven phrases. As a consequence the primary information is relegated in small print to a lower level. The summary style imposed by the software, using many abbreviations, makes the meaning confused and gives rise to ambiguity about some terms or emphasizes others, such as *significant*—used five times in the NASA presentation, with no statistical justification for the use of the adjective. Tuft considers that "pitch-style typography," the piling up of slogans, is completely inappropriate for a scientific report, and concludes that this formal graphic hierarchy is likely to lead to tragic consequences, particularly in very technical areas like aeronautics.[22] The board investigating the

shuttle disaster was indeed very critical on this point, condemn-
ing NASA's carelessness in the preparation of these reports:

> At many points during its investigation, the Board was surprised
> to receive similar presentation slides from NASA officials in
> place of technical reports. The Board views the endemic use of
> PowerPoint briefing slides instead of technical papers as an illus-
> tration of the problematic methods of technical communication
> at NASA.[23]

Although the obsession with lists is characteristic of Power-
Point, it is not limited to presentation software programs.
According to Didier L., a French pioneer of e-learning and head
of a training center: "It's a little like SMS or instant messaging, a mode of communication characterized by short phrases,
key words, and abbreviations, with no syntax, limiting any complexity or double meaning: objects become simple even though
reality is complex. It makes people feel safe, like a teddy bear.
And besides, we're a culture of channel-surfing, we shift rapidly from one idea to another, with no link, no logical construction." It is difficult in this connection not to think of Facebook
or Twitter as well, for which the favorite mode of expression is
also the list and the composition of ever more summary and la-
conic messages.

The logic of the list thus fits into a more general cognitive
ecosystem. It has become so preeminent that it has replaced the
traditional methods of organizing information. For example,
the most frequently used tool on the Web, the search engine,
has the distinctive characteristic of proposing a world in which
every occurrence is presented in the form of hierarchical lists.
The hierarchies are sometimes established by the purchase of
key words, as for Google, by which an advertiser can preempt

lists of words that will automatically be displayed once they are entered into the search engine. PowerPoint also enables us to measure the effects of changes in the means of access to knowledge and information that strengthen this "listed" (and paying) view of the world.

A "DISEMBODIED" DISCOURSE

With the increasing domination of the mass media, everyday language has gradually been infected with advertising slogans. As early as 1928, Sigmund Freud's American nephew Edward Bernays published a little handbook that legitimated the reign of propaganda in Western democracies in politics and business. "Modern propaganda is a consistent, enduring effort to create or shape events to influence the relations of the public to an enterprise, idea, or group."[24] Bernays offers a set of very effective recipes for any beginner in public relations.

From then on, a common and universal language became the utilitarian vector of communication and information, one of whose characteristics was to be naturally affirmative, positive, optimistic, and assertive. Simplicity of the message, mobility and plasticity of the media, speed of distribution, multiplicity of meanings, and standardization of images have become primary constituents of every communicative discourse.

PowerPoint is the ideal medium for this kind of discourse, which has to charm and mobilize while exploiting authority and competence. Pride in concision, the desire to simplify, the culture of the slogan—the advertising language of PowerPoint makes possible a fragmentation of meaning: no global vision, no chain of argument except the one induced by a sequence of unconnected words. In this perpetual channel-surfing, in which the eye picks up unconnected bits of information and fixes on a few words or images, meaning quickly becomes concentrated and then diluted. Writing effectively, quickly, and briefly is certainly not easy. But the last decade has seen the birth and coming to maturity of a generation of experts able with unusual dexterity to produce slides with their stripped-down syntax and automatic formulas. It is as though PowerPoint had engendered a specific and shifting language, like those created by SMS, chat rooms, and instant messaging.

The advertising language adopted by PowerPoint is based on a register that specialists call epideictic.[25] It is one of the three genres of oratory: the judicial accuses or defends, the deliberative advises for or against, and the epideictic praises or blames. The epideictic is addressed to the man in the street (in contrast to judges or a legislature); it is focused on the present and designed to "sell" a person or a product as being good or bad. This advertising-style discourse prefers to charm through description to induce action, create a reaction, or incite the audience. It thus creates utterances that do not need to be established, argued, demonstrated.[26]

Like advertising, PowerPoint presentations resort to hyperbole and amplification—you have to "oversell" through language. Hence rhetorical amplification "through an effect of derealization, makes it possible to take advantage of the dramatizing power of some expressions with no risk of being taken literally."[27] PowerPoint presentations are saturated with these amplifications: "*veritable* managerial evolution," "*profound* reform of capital allocation," "*major* evolution of our cost structure," "*complete* reversal of tendency." It is even not unusual to find some complacently asserting that they "have *the largest* distribution network in Asia," "carry out *the most important* financial operation of the last ten years," or made "*the most important* acquisition in our history."

This does not prevent PowerPoint from also playing on implication and allusion, which is no contradiction, because, like hyperbole, the recourse to ellipsis helps to smooth out all the rough edges in the presentation. Ellipsis, from the Greek *elleipsis* (a defect or incomplete figure), is a device consisting of removing words from a sentence that are necessary for its correct grammatical construction: "Out of a concern for economy and speed, the utterance is reduced to the minimum necessary for the message to be transmitted intelligibly."[28] It is thus an invitation to shortcuts and summaries.

For example, one finds in the institutional presentation of a major bank a series of "principles of action" expressed in a set of incomplete and even incomprehensible statements:

- Develop in profitability
- By applying our values that inspire the attitudes and principles of the management within the group
- Sustainable development

The format that requires concision also produces an absence of meaning: develop what, what are the inspiring values, and what is sustainable development doing here? These statements are in fact more interesting for what they don't say, what they leave in suspense, up to the discretion of the audience. The same thing goes for slogans like:

A platform turned toward growth

To master development costs on a competitive basis

Constant transformation to compensate for unfavorable factors

Pursue development by mastering risks

Consolidate profitability (cost containment)

In France, activity should remain at a high level.[29]

Some even feel obliged to explain in parentheses what is to be understood. This emphasis on shortcuts can produce ambiguity as to the meaning of certain formulations, or even completely empty words of their meaning.

The composition of PowerPoint slides requires other rhetorical devices of subtraction, such as asyndeton, the omission of connective terms where they would normally be used in a sentence,[30] as in "client-service or promise," "product offensive or range," "expansion of store network—25 new concept stores," "constant perimeter stable total production," "stable expedited 2007 production, with constant perimeter." All these are statements in which the juxtaposition of words with no logical connection can corrupt understanding, particularly if the medium of presentation is not accompanied with commentary.

This procedure omits copulas (to be), temporal conjunctions (before, after), or logical conjunctions (but, therefore). A common device in advertising language, asyndeton can have an expressive function that accentuates the assertive aspect of the action expressed. Entire presentations can, for example, set out sentences with no subject, no logical connections, no indication of interdependence, provoking in the reader an atomization of units of meaning that only the speaker can in the end coordinate. But the speaker often merely repeats the statements displayed, directly reproducing the disconnected and cumulative aspect of the presentation.

Euphemism is another device frequently used by the new

language of power. This major element in economic and political Newspeak is also a central device in "correct powerpointing." Euphemism is an "attenuation of the expression in relation to the information conveyed. . . . It is used, in argument or in fiction, whenever it is convenient to mask, through attenuation or veiling, a given reality; receivers (listeners or readers) are always capable of understanding correctly or not."[31] In Éric Hazan's view, euphemization makes it possible to skirt the meaning of a problem or an expression—for instance, the expression *social partners** makes it possible to dispose of the idea of conflict, and the term *privatization* is intended to create the impression that the private individual is being given back what the state had taken from him, while the opposite is what is happening.

In institutional presentations of annual earnings, in particular, the device turns out to be very practical, because the context and the audience—management, peers, shareholders, analysts, reporters—requires soothing, all-purpose communication and politically correct discourse. Euphemization strategies make it possible to smooth things over. According to an attentive observer of these presentations: "It is a matter of manipulating words in such a way that they end up changing their original meaning and declaring in a gentle and light way truths that are hard to say to an audience, the shareholders of whom these bosses are in a sense the 'employees' and who are playing with the shareholders' savings." The analysis of a presentation intended for the small shareholders of Eurotunnel provides an enlightening example. A private Anglo-French company that manages the channel tunnel inaugurated in June 1994, Eurotunnel was by 1997 experiencing many financial difficulties, caused primarily by construction and

---

* Commonly used in French to denote management and labor (translator).

maintenance cost overruns as well as by a lower volume of traffic than initial studies had predicted. Whereas Eurotunnel reached its highest share price in 1989 (more than €27), it collapsed in succeeding years, reaching €0.34 in 2003; that year, the Autorité des Marchés Financiers went so far as to suspend trading in the company's shares.

When it presented its 2004 earnings report on April 26, 2005, Eurotunnel was still in a difficult position. Cross-channel traffic was still below expectations, and the company referred to many "disputes," detailed in the presentation,[32] in particular with governments but also with shareholders, primarily small shareholders (nearly 70 percent of the company's capital), to whom the company announced the establishment of shareholder committees designed to "facilitate communication between company and shareholders."[33]

The company had therefore decided to implement a new strategy, summarized in a slide:

- Counter the decline in revenue.
- Improve the company's performance.
- Handle the social impact.

The first line resorts yet again to the military lexicon. Counter, but how? In general by raising fares, which can be guessed from the subhead ("new adjusted fare schedule"). Rather than stating it openly, it is preferable to give the discourse a positive slant by the use of euphemism, as one learns in every public relations agency.

The next line—"Improve the company's performance"—is a commonplace in this type of presentation that calls on the notions of commercial competitiveness and efficiency. This often means something like "reorganization," "simplification of processes," "drastic reduction in overhead," and finally "restructuring plans."

The last line speaks of handling "the social impact," a vague expression that can range from simple reorganization of departments to the implementation of a restructuring plan, including dismissals, reclassifications, training programs, and dozens, hundreds, or even thousands of people forced to change job, status, address, and so on.

With an apparent concern for transparency, PowerPoint thus makes it possible to present "strong" and precise messages, while it is only displaying its aversion to calling a spade a spade. Proving its determined ambivalence, the software program communicates with hesitation and even hypocrisy while giving the impression of revealing all.

WHO IS SPEAKING?

In the framework of these strategies of evasion and circumvention, other methods, such as reported speech and quotation, are also used.

As in any talk, quotation is an easy way to enrich the presentation. It operates as an example and a picture: it shows, summons an external position, a commitment made by a personality—generally a consensual figure—who often has little to do with the presenter and those he represents.

Uses of quotation for various purposes enable us to sketch a rough typology:

• The quotation of conviction, or programmatic quotation. Probably the most frequently used, this is the slogan, often the expression of the head of the company or of a famous corporate leader, statesman, or management guru. Closely related, the formulaic quotation, axiom, received truth, proverb, or profession of faith, derives all its legitimacy from quotation marks.

• The ironic quotation. With its deflating comedy, irony paradoxically makes it possible to strengthen a demonstration. These witticisms—a specialty of showmen, particularly Americans—generally come from a pantheon of personalities (and often Web sites that compile undocumented quotations and organize them according to major themes) like Winston Churchill and Albert Einstein, or comic writers like Woody Allen and Groucho Marx.

• The "expressive" quotation. Used so as to be retained, like a song tune. This is a creation of the presenter that can function simultaneously as a poetic image and a slogan; for example, in *An Inconvenient Truth*, Al Gore (see chapter 5) intones, simultaneously with its appearance on the screen, the following sentence: "We are witnessing a collision between our civilization and the Earth."[34]

• The paradoxical, provocative quotation. To ridicule the opposing position, the speaker can quote the arguments offered by opponents or comments from the press.

• The quotation of other slides. There is nothing better than intentional cutting and pasting—not concealed, as it usually is—to reveal mistakes or to criticize or contradict competing statements;

• A verbatim. This is a cliché of every presentation—particularly in organizations that conduct qualitative studies and opinion surveys, such as TNS, BVA, or IPSOS. In the world of marketing and the media, a *verbatim* is "made up of all the words and phrases used by a population in a survey or when individuals spontaneously address a company (mail, telephone, e-mail)."[35]

Verbatim has become the generic term to designate any testimonial language reproduced in opinion or consumer surveys, whether used to articulate confidence ("I feel full of resources, capable of doing things") or as an element of reconstitution, words used as evidence, as in focus groups ("I like to mix old objects with more modern ones"). This culture of reported speech, testimony, the celebrated "ordinary" speech, has developed considerably in the last fifteen or twenty years. The language of the woman in the street, the voice of the customer, has acquired unquestionable legitimacy in the eyes of marketers: it is the gospel, the authenticated verdict, the certified judgment. In a world where truth comes from "the field," where it is necessary to cultivate proximity and empathy, the verbatim becomes a weighty shock argument. One consultant explains: "We cannot consider giving a client a report of a study, without scattering some verbatims thorough it that corroborate, systematically validate our conclusions and recommendations." This form of reported speech enables the author of the report to surreptitiously evade responsibility by allowing him to rely on the words of the witness-king.

PowerPoint presentations, supported by these rhetorical strategies, are largely based on a logic of authority. Quotation, verbatims, slogans, infinitive forms: all elements of speech that make it possible to hit hard, to persuade, to impose a discourse supported by a closed visual system and an oral and gestural delivery that functions almost as a redundant layer.

At this stage, the most striking thing is the perversity of this discursive system. PowerPoint implies an idea of exchange and debate, interactivity, whereas all its language, fragmented and elliptical, encourages only slogans, commands, and authority. The software is also supposed to enable the individual to express creativity and affirm autonomy, but this goal is hindered by an extremely formalized framework in which the effacement of the speaker is manifest and the neutrality of the statements transforms personal expression into all-purpose language that has always already been legitimated.

4

FROM OBFUSCATION TO FALSIFICATION

➡

A PowerPoint presentation appeals primarily to visual perception: it is based on a representational framework; it is projected
or printed; it requires a graphic organization of information; it
calls for following rules of readability; it calls on graphs, diagrams, and tables; and last but not least, it includes increasing
numbers of photographs, illustrations, and even videos.

The presentation conforms to very specific, often "operational," goals of distribution, sharing, and information exchange.
Its relationship to graphs and images is therefore functional.
Images are "designed according to a conscious or intuitive code
and carried on a physical medium with the intention of communicating specific information."[1]

After a brief consideration of the dominance of the screen
and of special effects on our perception and our visual means
of acquiring information, I will analyze a medical presentation.
This example will make it possible to observe how graphs and
diagrams are used in the scientific world, which, it is legitimate
to assume, obeys the most rigorous standards. It will also enable us to see how visual devices, under various constraints, are
often cobbled together deceptively and sometimes even diverted

from their initial purpose. For in the majority of PowerPoint presentations, graphic devices, whose declared purpose is to illustrate a demonstration, finally obscure and falsify matters. It is as though the exuberance of special effects and the software's ease of graphic creation produced exactly the opposite of what was aimed for.

SCREENS AND LANDSCAPES

Louise R. is a researcher in a major French opinion survey institute. When asked about her use of PowerPoint, she recounted this experience with complete spontaneity:

> In the course of my professional experience, I have undergone a curious shift. As a student, I wrote on sheets of A4 paper in Page mode. Today, I write by hand in Landscape format as though I were unconsciously making slides. It structures my thinking. I even go so far as to draw frames, strips, lines. I have the impression that the program makes me more precise, more implacable. No one can prove that what I have written is false. By using the whole page, one asserts that the truth is constructed like that.

Does that mean that the landscape format of PowerPoint produces cognitive effects that even condition a way of thinking and its formal expression? In any event, a major American investment bank indulged in "vice" to the extent of preparing PowerPoint-type presentations in landscape format, but using Word. Word documents are thus manipulated to obtain certain visual, tabular, and sequential effects, as with PowerPoint, but with fewer limitations on textual content.

Design and writing in PowerPoint, like the reading and visualization of most documents, are now carried out in the majority of cases through a screen. The screen is the universal format of all communication, increasingly cannibalizing the usual vertical format of reading. Television, cinema, telephone, computers, e-readers, medical imagery, or optical equipment—virtually all production, circulation, and sharing of knowledge can be conceived of only as confined to a screen, tiny or gigantic.

Unlike paper, the primary medium for manuscripts, books, and drawings, the screen provides the obvious advantage of mobility in an age when information has to be quick, modifiable, transmittable, and consultable everywhere:

> That is the principle of the screen: it is interchangeable, substitutable for another for the information that it displays. . . . Its fluidity and liquefaction take the place of the mobility of the traditional medium for writing, paper. . . . The screen neutralizes the materiality of the mark and makes its displacement easy. . . . The screen is free and amnesiac.[2]

This "rectangular" view of the world does not, of course, date from the invention of HDTV and the PC but from the Renaissance.[3] The representation of space changed; the frame of the painting became a "window opening onto the world," the painting an instrument of knowledge. From that time forward, the view of the real world was associated with the rectangular form of framing. "The rectangle is a concise, neutral, abstract form that tends to disappear by creating a 'transparent' arrangement that naturalizes the appearance of the image. The rectangular form is also a rational form that makes efficient use of media by taking its place in an economy of formats."[4] Because of this limitation, vision became more ductile and more available. Because of the laws of perspective, which imposed standards of balance and stability, the rectangular frame instituted a fictitious form of neutrality (that was denounced by all artistic avant-gardes from the late nineteenth century onward). With the emergence of photography, followed by the invention of mass reproduction, this format was identified with looking: the rectangle became the universal frame for the visual field.

The screen provides a novel space for reading: deciphering takes place instantaneously and globally, continuously and autonomously; decoding is no longer subject to chronology, the sequence of reading page after page. The screen makes it possible, globally, synchronously, and continuously to identify separate, confused, and discontinuous elements. With the frame as elementary constituent, PowerPoint forces one to create pages as so many accumulations of screens. The various design models are constructed on the basis of frames to be adjusted, displaced, piled up, and so on. Texts, images, drawings, and graphs are inserted within strict limits.

This perpetual framing of signs obviously has effects on meaning and thinking. For the templates, as we have seen, force one to be brief and elliptical. Not to mention automatic design models and templates that impose (literally) a page design and therefore the volume and the form of the content. To construct a slide, each action is determined by a frame within which the content is included: "Click to add a title, text, then double click to add a graph, an image from the library, a hierarchical chart." The slide becomes a kind of Lego toy in which one arranges frames and images, often somewhat at random and subject to size constraints.

In a chapter of his book titled "Managerial Unreadability," Christian Morel speaks of an "office version of Russian dolls" to characterize PowerPoint.[5] The sociologist observes that, contrary to its intention, the tool tends to limit readability, especially by reducing the size of the reading space: the software diminishes the useful surface of the document during the design phase. The systematic use of data entry forms and frames forces one to limit words, to reduce font size, and hence to diminish readability. And the importation of objects, particularly Excel spreadsheets and graphs, themselves reduced before transfer, makes slides even more unreadable. Christian Morel concludes: "We are faced with a tool as widely distributed as refrigerators, for example, and whose widely used functionalities seem determined to largely erode its principal function, readability. It's almost as though refrigerators contained functionalities that gradually abolished the function of refrigerating."[6]

Screen writing by definition, PowerPoint presentations also subject our viewing to physiological constraints. Visual perception is a complex organic and mental operation that integrates physiological factors along with cultural elements linked to the spectator's environment: one sees and perceives clearly what one knows, what one can name, classify, represent, describe. Viewing takes place in three stages: sensory—one focuses on and grasps the object; perceptual—one arranges and organizes the information (notably according to the laws of gestalt);[7] and cognitive—one interprets the object according to various codes. The visual field of an individual generally encompasses 200 degrees. Central, or foveolate, vision, which covers only 2 degrees, is the clearest: everything outside this field is imprecise—one distinguishes only masses and movements. This central vision is very acute and makes it possible to clearly distinguish colors, light intensities, and forms.

An average reader can read two hundred words a minute. Working memory implemented in reading enables one to retain between seven and ten word in a few seconds. Generally speaking, human memory capacity spans seven elements.[8] The eyes do not read letter by letter but group them in small packets: they constantly scan, alternating fixation and movement. The effort can produce fatigue and cognitive overload, especially if texts are too small in relation to the distance from spectators, interline spacing is not large enough, typography is not appropriate, or colors of text and background are not properly adjusted. Readers end up focusing on a few words that stand out, according to the law of minimum effort. Dan Sperber and Deirdre Wilson consider that the more cognitive effect an item of information produces on the recipient, the more relevant the recipient will find it; conversely, the more effort required, the less relevant it will seem.[9]

Thus, contrary to its stated goals, a PowerPoint projection can produce confusion and visual fatigue that is often increased by the dim light in projection rooms. Reading on a screen is an activity that calls upon many physiological and cognitive resources and can therefore quickly overtax the audience. Indeed, every presentation calls on the spectators to accomplish simultaneously and/or successively four complex cognitive operations: the audience must distinguish, decipher, understand and interpret, and finally believe and accept. The first two operations put in play common cognitive resources. The two following call on different capacities of visual perception. And it is precisely the fact of mixing all these visual activities that makes the reading of PowerPoint a difficult exercise, especially if the visual ergonomics is not optimal and the language is confused.

Over the last ten years, European and American studies have continually measured the degree of readability and effectiveness of PowerPoint presentations. Dave Paradi, author of a PowerPoint guide, reports on a survey of 688 people conducted on the Internet in 2007 and intended to identify the major sources of boredom when viewing a presentation.[10] Far in front is the inept speaker who reads his slides (62 percent), followed by texts in small typefaces (46.9 percent), bad choice of colors (42.6 percent), and complete sentences in place of bullet lists (39.1 percent).[11] This confirms, incidentally that the bullet point is indeed the soul of PowerPoint and that those who try to get away from this mode of exposition, whose perils we have seen, are in danger of missing their target.

DISINFORMATION ABOUT A PANDEMIC

Aside from the physiological conditions of visibility and readability, the use of visuals in PowerPoint, though the source of its success, poses deeper problems. The easy integration into PowerPoint of images and graphs can considerably alter the quality of the information, its validity, or even its credibility, especially in fields that require the greatest precision.

In the first months of 2009, the public health authorities of many Western countries began to broadcast warnings about a particularly virulent and threatening flu virus, H1N1. As a result, with the help of a press campaign, real anxiety gripped public opinion and spread to many institutions. Major international companies implemented business continuity plans (BCP), procedures enabling them to continue operations and to "provide the same service to their clients in case of a major disaster," specifically an epidemic.

At meetings of BCP committees in companies around the world, PowerPoint presentations proliferated, describing "new threats of infection," "flu types," "the flu pandemic," "swine flu," "Mexican flu," and so on.[12]

The presentation analyzed here was given in companies during the first quarter of 2009 by a major French hospital establishment. Limited to a dozen slides,[13] it served as the basis for meetings intended to inform managers—who might play a role

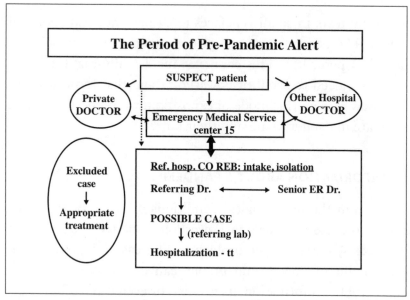

FIGURE 1 The choice of design elements, typefaces, colors, and layout creates confusion and muddles the message.

in the event of an established pandemic and the triggering of a BCP—about the disease in a pedagogical way.

All the design choices are questionable from the outset in terms of readability. The visual organization is haphazard; the choice of typography, improper; and the choice of images, fanciful. Confusion reigns and will increase as the dozen slides succeed one another.

The heterogeneity of the typography, for example, transforms an institutional presentation emanating from a public health establishment into a rough, amateurish graphic montage. Disparate typography leads to capricious discourse, false argument, and heterogeneous information.

The Web is full of collections of advice (often funny) on the traps to be avoided in preparing a presentation. There are even some comic routines[14] making fun of unreadable slides, common spelling mistakes, messy or overly complex design, and laughable animations. These routines rightly discredit the ubiquitous and often superfluous use of the visual possibilities of the program.

More serious sites provide tutorials giving the elementary rules of typography and the organization of slides, along with hints for dramatic presentation. In the face of the multiplicity of effects made possible by the program, these methods consist, neither more nor less, of imposing new rules and new standards more in keeping with the layout of the slide. These standards of presentation, particularly with respect to design, also establish new prescriptions reproduced in one presentation after another until they become not just design models but frameworks of thinking. This is again the great paradox of PowerPoint: it is the favored medium for the new ideology of creativity in business while producing very controlling (and impoverishing) frames and forms of organization and thinking.

Indeed, some experts in PowerPoint can be implacable. For instance, one of the most famous, Guy Kawasaki, has propounded the 10/20/30 rule:

> A PowerPoint presentation should have ten slides, last no more than twenty minutes, and contain no font smaller than thirty points. . . . Ten is the optimal number of slides in a PowerPoint presentation because a normal human being cannot comprehend more than ten concepts in a meeting. . . . If you must use more than ten slides to explain your business, you probably don't have a business. . . . You should give your ten slides in twenty minutes. Sure, you have an hour time slot, but you're using a Windows laptop, so it will take forty minutes to make it work with the projector. Even if setup goes perfectly, people will arrive late and have to leave early. . . . Force yourself to use no font smaller than thirty points. I guarantee it will make your presentations

better, because it requires you to find the most salient points and to know how to explain them well. If "thirty points," is too dogmatic, then I offer you an algorithm: find out the age of the oldest person in your audience and divide it by two. That's your optimal font size.[15]

This style, mixing the appearance of a recipe, numerical mnemonic devices, practical advice, an ironic tone, and advertising language, is quite typical of the form adopted by the authors of this kind of literature. Some, like Nancy Duarte, add a more affective touch, emotional or human. Garr Reynolds shows a more pronounced inclination for elegance and purity of design, while Seth Godin is more focused on commercial pragmatism and efficiency. But while criticizing naive uses of the program, these heavyweights of presentation, who are salespeople of expertise on the subject, are instituting new models of communication that exploit the many perverse effects of the language of PowerPoint, particularly the propensity toward simplification, the "weight of words and the shock of photographs," the preponderance of form over content, the dictatorship of fleeting memory, quick comic effect, and a whole rhetorical mechanism that is more exhibitionist than argumentative.

The H1N1 presentation raises questions about the use of graphs and diagrams, ubiquitous in the design language of PowerPoint. The second slide in the presentation offers a diagram that is rather common in the repertory of graphs: a curve with two axes—the x-axis shows the time in years, from one to ten and beyond (thirty?); the y-axis has two scales of value written vertically.

It is immediately apparent that location tools are imprecise and perfunctory. A curve and a yellow straight dotted line indicate a pandemic peak in the first year, but what is the unit

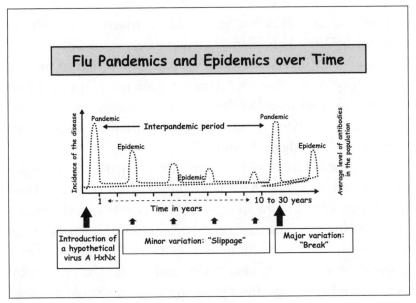

FIGURE 2   (H1N1): An imprecise use of a graph.

of measurement for the "incidence of the disease"? Four dotted peaks decreasing in size probably indicate a decline in epidemics, until after ten to thirty years (no way of telling), there is a new pandemic peak. No scale or unit enables the viewer to measure the values being compared concretely and with any precision. Between the two pandemic peaks, a yellow arrow indicates the period between the two pandemics; beneath the y-axis, the viewer does not know what the red dotted arrow indicates. There are two final indications in the frame: "Slippage" and "Break." The graph is titled "Flu pandemics and epidemics over time."

This is a typical example of the kind of enigmatic diagram that adorns millions of slides around the world every day. Not only does this graph not meet any standards governing the use of diagrams, but also it shows the extent to which, on the pretext of prettifying, very serious people begin to forget the most elementary precision about very serious subjects.

Precision in graphs is a huge field, to which Jacques Bertin devoted his life. This French cartographer, who died in 2010, produced considerable work on the use and design of graphic information tools: "Graphic representation is a part of the fundamental sign systems that humanity has constructed to retain, understand, and communicate the observations necessary for its survival and the life of the mind."[16]

Bertin established rules of composition for the three categories he analyzed. The *diagram* establishes relationships among components and groups all representations into several subcategories, as in histograms, curves, bar diagrams, circular diagrams (pie charts), diagrams with more than two non-orthogonal axes (radar or spider charts), cloud plots, and so on. The *network* establishes relationships among elements of a single component, as in genealogical trees, organization charts, road networks, flow charts, algorithms, and so on. The *map* represents a visible space, a profile, an assemblage, a geographical space. To these three categories must be added the *outline*, a simplified and functional figure which is more abstract than the diagram.

Graphic communication in Bertin's view, as a monosemic system,[17] requires rigor and precision, following the model of mathematics. Bertin constructed a system making it possible to deploy rigorous graphic representations so as to fulfill three essential functions: memorization, understanding, and communication, the original goals of PowerPoint.

Graphic communication offers the advantage of not being subject to the linear rules of written and oral discourse. It offers the possibility of grasping information as a whole with its context, treating it in parallel rather than sequentially, of not necessarily being fixed in advance, and of expressing emotion (like emoticons in e-mails and text messages). Visual perception enables one to make decisions without going through the filter of language, without translation into speech.

A rather young marketing director in a cyber commerce company, Arthur M. was an engineer before switching to communication. He states:

> As an engineer, one is very graphic, one tends to translate everything into sketches, drawings, without too many words. With graphs, you don't confuse your audience, you go right to the essential. Writing contains more ambiguities because words and sentences have several meanings, whereas an outline is simple, quick, and direct.

This analysis is confirmed by another computer consultant: "A drawing is a reflection of the consultant's thinking, and he uses it as the most generic possible medium to have his ideas flow quickly and be rapidly shared by a collection of individuals from different backgrounds."

Indeed, graphic representation offers multiple possibilities in all areas of activity: describing a phenomenon, comparing data, connecting notions, representing an organization, sketching flows, indicating assemblages, and so on. Diagrams and graphs bring to the fore information that would not be so apparent if other systems of meaning were used: through its more global vision, its more direct presentation of anomalies, its simplifying function, its reproducibility, graphic representation greatly facilitates communication while also taking on a kind of scientific veneer.

But the use of graphic communication opens the way to all kinds of manipulations. Before launching a vigorous attack on PowerPoint, Edward Tufte had built his success in the 1980s[18] by publishing books denouncing the virtually fraudulent use of graphs in contemporary media and the way one can make numbers lie through graphs.[19] Tufte analyzes the distortions committed either in the name of esthetics and graphic ease or to dress up unfavorable information, radically changing our perception of the underlying data.

He refers in particular to graphs (histograms or curves) establishing year by year comparisons, which are frequently used in economics, finance, and contemporary media (out of four thousand graphs from fifteen newspapers and magazines between 1974 and 1980, Tufte notes that 75 percent of them are diagrams of this type). It appears that graphic designers often doctor the shape of the data to accent a progression or to hide a decline. For example, they play with the proportions of data representation, illustrating the differences in completely capricious ways.[20]

In the 1980s and 1990s, researchers demonstrated that diagrams offered by companies in circumstances where it was legitimate to expect precision were often imprecise and sometimes incorrect.[21] Management professor Éric Maton, for example, has established in detail how experts in financial communication create distortions in graphic representations by such devices as manipulating the slope of curves, "inducing an underestimation of the positive variation in data."[22] He remarks that the growing pressure of shareholders (particularly institutional shareholders) in the 1990s led companies to publish quarterly results that could be read quickly, although no rules of graphic representation were promulgated,[23] despite the fact that all financial information is now heavily regulated.

In order to make the principal numbers (the "key numbers") as attractive as possible, designers can use various devices. They favor, for example, three-dimensional bar diagrams, on occasion stylizing the bars in the form of the company's leading products. This is known as "impression management": the idea is to give a good impression graphically according to four factors: "the selectivity of variables represented, the distortion of proportions, the choice of a favorable slope, and the improvement of the presentation."[24]

Éric Maton denounces French companies, half of whose annual reports contain "falsified" diagrams, although he recognizes that they are subject to growing pressure from shareholders, to whom they owe timely information, as well as continual and necessary relationships with more and more demanding financial analysts:

> In these circumstances, diagrams play an important role. Their power is linked to a psychological phenomenon identified as the "halo effect." If one shows, at the beginning of an annual report or in PowerPoint documents in a presentation of financial data, diagrams presenting the data in a good light, there is an appreciable risk that the report as a whole will be read or the presentation heard with a positive preconception that will influence judgment on the other information provided.[25]

An essential information tool for many organizations, the graphic representation of numerical information, originally decked out in a whole scientific and technical apparatus, has been transformed, by means of an astute esthetic costume, into an adulterated but exhilarating message for its audience, particularly shareholders. Thanks to impression management, the company offers its audience an acceptable discourse through "flattering graphic representations." Of course, the question of the precision and relevance of graphic representations did not appear with PowerPoint, but the spread of their use thanks to the ruling program has tended to normalize or even to amplify a slightly illicit way of producing favorable graphs in organizations. Financial results, an epidemiological curve, implementation of a mobile action plan, rollout of a product, presentation of a new organization: in industry, services, or the military, in health or education, in the public and private sectors, PowerPoint graphic language, under cover of its richness and ease of use, produces powerful perverse effects.

IMAGES THAT UNDERMINE CREDIBILITY

The diagrams and graphs presented by the medical corps about H1N1 flu may seem a blunder due to inexperience, but what about images? It is difficult today to imagine even a modest presentation without the inclusion of an image, a drawing, a graphic element. Everyone considers it indispensable to add a little animation to a serious world and especially a bit of his or her personality and esthetic sense. For fans of domestic slides, the use of professional PowerPoint becomes a moment of pure creative freedom, especially because the thoughtless use of images is ubiquitous in everyday life, as though every message had to be illustrated, decorated, accented by an image, in conformity with the saying, A picture is worth a thousand words. Unfortunately, this widespread injunction to illustrate usually produces ridiculous effects and extravagant results.

From a reading of the last three H1N1 slides, one has to recognize that an illustration can have devastating effects on the credibility of the information presented.

They are bullet lists illustrated by snapshots as trivial as they are tacky: the first slide presents a chronology of various viruses in the form of a list adorned with a photograph of ambulance drivers from the early twentieth century. One might guess the meaning of this reference if one remembers that the most deadly flu epidemic took place early in the century and if one assumes that the faded charm of the image is intended to lighten the subject. But one could just as well interpret this photograph as a disguised criticism of the ridiculous resources provided by the public health authorities.

This is one of the first equivocations or uncertainties put in play by the use of figurative images and photographs in presentations: unlike a diagram, which theoretically can have only one meaning, an illustration or photograph contains a multiplicity of possible meanings (polysemy) depending on the context: the subject, place, society, history, audience, and so on, and its arrangement in the space represented.

In a PowerPoint presentation, an illustration or photograph can, along the lines of its journalistic use or use as a quotation (see the preceding chapter), meet several goals: It can be *informative*, illustrating and supporting a proposition. In that case, the iconographic document provides nonredundant additional information. It can be *esthetic* or *decorative*. To prettify, one adds to the messages an image that the designer believes will embellish his remarks. This use is very dangerous, because the tastes of the audience are often heterogeneous. It can be *documentary*. Beyond information, the designer of the presentation may have to provide proof of a fact, describe a project, certify a piece of information, or explain a procedure. It can be *rhetorical*. The image is used as a stylistic figure in the speech, e.g., common metaphor of schematic forms (tree, planets, targets, and so on). The analogy can be symbolic and cultural, becoming the vector of an idea, an atmosphere, a notion, a brand. Or the graphic can be *amusing*. The use of comic illustrations is also risky, humor being such an individual matter.

In the H1N1 presentation, one slide presents the means of transmission of the disease, particularly transportation. What

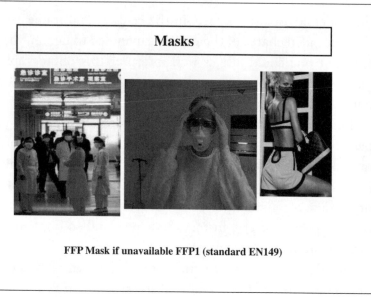

FIGURE 3 Spectacle or information?

images are chosen to illustrate it? A train, a truck, a canoe—who would have thought of that? Concluding from that that flu is communicable by canoe is a stretch. This kind of decorative image produces only noise, diverting attention, which can turn out to be fatal if the message is lacking in clarity.

The Masks slide presents three photographs: one of hospital employees wearing masks in a Chinese establishment, a second probably of a colleague in the hospital, and finally a model shot from behind at a three-quarter angle, very lightly dressed in a short skirt and bra and displaying a bag and a splendid Louis Vuitton mask.

The most cursory search for images on Google, while providing many images of Asian origin (the bird flu of a few years ago had aftereffects, particularly in image banks), would have been able to meet documentary needs at modest cost, particularly because the only real information is at the bottom of the slide:

Reorganize

- **Protect Personnel +++**
- **Protection of Families??**
- **Receiving clients and visitors**
- **Maintaining Goals +++ f(sectors)**
- **Maintain Activities at their highest level: Anticipations**
- **f(Absenteeism):**

> **(Illness, Fear, Right to withdraw, Traffic difficulties, Schools-Daycare centers)**

FIGURE 4 The weight of words or the shock of photographs?

"FFP2 Mask if unavailable FFP1 (standard EN 149)." This is neither a code nor a rebus but references to masks approved by the medical establishment.

Once again the use of superfluous images provokes perplexity. It is not so much the requirements of the discourse that demand the image, but rather the customary practice of the tool that seems to *impose* the illustration, even if it is useless. Technical ease, as it were, creates an obligation to decorate that leads to incongruities, which make us think, for example, that Louis Vuitton produced a line of antiflu masks especially for the event.

The last image of the presentation is a slide under the title Reorganize: a warship in the shadows simply lit up by an explosion, the text accompanying the slide speaking of personnel, family, clients, and visitors, of absenteeism and schools. In a word, one can hardly see a connection to the military image if it is not to make the public aware of the danger and the importance of measures to be taken, by frightening it with this image of warfare.

The picture of a warship or a storm-tossed vessel is one of the many analogical-iconographic clichés that flourish in presentations, particularly in businesses, in times of crisis. Take the following anecdote about an international financial company. Preparing the presentation of the strategic plan, a manager in charge of strategy, a former consultant, focused on the graphic design that he wanted to present to the members of his management committee. An expert in often very complex slides with a good deal of content, the strategist looked for the powerful and significant image that would strike his audience on the introductory page. He wanted to send the managers a "strong message" about the company's ability to successfully go through a troubled period. An expressive photograph of a storm-tossed ship combined with an old stylized compass against a background of a stock-market trading floor, and the trick was done.

It is likely that the preparation of this superficial metaphor with esthetic and emotional purposes took some time—looking for the image, reworking it, setting it with the title, formatting, and so on—that could have been used either to refine the strategic analysis or to work on the presentation as a whole. And for the audience, it is likely that the pretty picture served the argument only by placing them in a passive position as receivers. It is a good bet that the audience had a better memory of the striking image than of an unreadable table that was nonetheless essential because it summarized the strategic actions to be implemented in the coming years. The basic purpose of the image was certainly to touch the audience, to offer them a comforting starting point that would distract, intrigue, and move them, but that risked turning their attention away from the message to be retained.

The impulse toward "artistic" creation and the taste for exhibition that PowerPoint encourages drive designers to include visuals to charm their audience. In the majority of cases, these visuals are drawn from their own stocks, from their company's image banks, or from the inexhaustible copyright-free stores of image banks. Although it is easy to find the right photograph by typing on Google Images or other image banks key words such as "childhood disease," "financial crisis," or "H1N1 flu," it seems much more difficult to avoid clichés, well-known, standardized, and politically correct visuals.

Perhaps worst is the use of the visuals included with PowerPoint, clip art famous around the world. A former graphic designer at Microsoft, Cathleen Belleville worked on the program from 1989 to 1995. She describes her surprise at discovering a few years later that the numerous drawings she had created to give ideas to presentation designers had become veritable icons of modern business,[26] particularly the "screen beans," androgynous stick figures, one of the most famous of which is the figure with a light bulb above its head.[27] Another figure scratching its head in puzzlement under a question mark has become so popular that a New York corporate lawyer, a regular user of PowerPoint, claims to have never seen a presentation without it. Belleville says she has seen her screen beans around the world, reproduced on baseball caps, even ten feet high in a Hamburg bank.

It would be pointless to present an inventory of surrealistic clipart available in various versions of the program. The most striking fact is that these illustrations often turn out to be inappropriate to any setting other than the United States: to represent the theme of sports, the choice is hockey, American football, or baseball. Some of the associations between theme and image are also surprising: in the category government, one finds handcuffs and a tank; in the vague category professional activity, one finds the picture of a deacon; the children category contains a church, and so on.

Some users are fond of one of the playful functionalities of PowerPoint, animations. These gadgets—for example making the text appear very gradually, or in blocks, illustrations at top or bottom and sometimes with sound—are commonly used by neophytes, who find them amusing and therefore effective.

But these animations are uniformly rejected by marketing, finance, and technology professionals, for various reasons, ranging from their tackiness and their cheap appearance to their excess consumption of time. "It's amusing, at a stretch, for family slide shows at home," according to a young advertising executive. "Logically, an animation should be an effective way to present processes such as weather events, electric circuits, biological regulatory systems, or mechanical arrangements. . . . The literature reports many cases in which animation did not produce the expected benefits."[28] Animation can be of value when it describes complex processes or operations. But the primary problem is that animation often diverts the attention of the audience from the content to the effect: it is no longer the speech that is important; the animation transports the audience. An architect comments on an animation about career choices for *lycée* students after graduation: "A stylized hand traced the arguments one by one, as though with a thread. I was fascinated by the hand and the threads. And I didn't read the text at all." With the pretext of decorating, one mystifies.

Once again, analysis of the uses of PowerPoint reveals a paradox: whereas the program provides the user with an impressive palette of graphic tools and an almost unlimited capacity to integrate multimedia elements, the results obtained are often unreadable, incomprehensible, and inelegant.

A presentation tool should in principle facilitate the exchange of information. Through its graphic prolixity, however, PowerPoint gives rise to obscurity, confusion, and cognitive fatigue. Moreover, the worldwide use of unreliable or doctored graphs and diagrams engenders doubt about the validity of a discourse that has been given a layout intended to ensure a form of legitimacy. Finally, the proliferation of images responding to an "esthetic" demand pollutes the argument. Emotion takes primacy over reason, exhibition over speech, spectacle over logic.

5

A TOTAL SPECTACLE

➡

A PowerPoint presentation is far from being limited to a juxtaposition of signs (words and images) projected onto a screen in front of an audience of whatever size. It has a third essential component: performance, direct presentation. For a presentation is an event, run by one or more individuals who, to make their points, rely on a combination of different media dispensed by an array of technologies.

Hence an oral presentation is a performance that requires staging and a setting. From a small meeting room for discussing a project with a few colleagues to an auditorium seating ten thousand for the annual convention of a giant cosmetics company, every presentation has to comply with a set of constraints— subject, place, material, time, performers—and customs whose primary purpose remains to direct the attention of an audience to information that it is supposed to take in, understand, and spread.

As has already been mentioned, PowerPoint has become in a decade the principal medium for any public oral presentation. What is of interest here is not the performance, the talent, or the charisma (all obviously variable) of the speakers, but rather the intrinsic capacity of the PowerPoint system to transform a simple oral presentation into a veritable exhibit mixing narration, spectacle, and dramaturgy.

All the sophisticated techniques developed over the centuries to exchange information, share skills, persuade others of the correctness of a decision, support particular groups, or mobilize people for action have given way before a huge accumulation of spectacle, in which one has to move fast, look good, and come on strong. Old techniques of debating or lecturing have been erased in favor of devices that favor a contest of technical and graphic quality and rhetorical and theatrical skill. A presentation has become a total spectacle.

To bring out the power of this new means of communication in public, I will describe the basic presentation at work in a sector that feasts on presentations, then discuss two examples that indicate the extent to which PowerPoint, originally conceived to produce professional presentations, has become in a few years a weapon of mass diffusion of the planetary spectacle.

FROM MEETING TO SHOW

With the spread of PowerPoint in organizations, the characteristics of the meeting have evolved. The usual work meeting has gone through profound changes due to the ubiquitous mediation of the tool.

Under the term company events, the sociologist Gérald Gaglio has grouped these "meetings between employees of different levels (meetings involving a 'procedure,' seminars, committees, conventions, assemblies)." He sets out a first typology specific to companies.

The *presentation-report* "is intended to draw up a balance sheet at a given moment, to show an immediate superior, colleagues, or counterparts the outcome of work completed or in progress. With a primarily informative aim, the presentation-report also contains an outline of future work" and "is principally concerned with projects (entire or segments)."

The *organizational presentation* is addressed to a larger audience, often higher up in the hierarchy. "Dealing with complex subjects that involve various departments in the company, it requires extra efforts of translation and concision compared to the first type, such as a precise reminder of the context or of definitions at the beginning of the presentation."[1]

The *presentation in progress*, "provisional, to be supplemented, not stabilized . . . provides a mixture of oral presentation, previously prepared digital slides, and 'live' correction and additions by the audience under the direction of a leader. Supplementing, prioritizing, 'validating' elements of the text, or arriving at a preliminary draft of a document by launching a subject (brainstorming, creative workshop) are proceedings that take place then."[2]

Originally for communicating and exchanging information, these meetings are now embellished with stagecraft that transforms them into creative sessions closer to participatory training than to a highly organized and hierarchical project meeting. Even as it is in preparation, the meeting with media support can stimulate collective or collaborative work. A slide becomes an element on which everyone can work, changing, redoing, copying, transmitting it, and so on, making possible an extension of the act of writing. And this situation can also be replayed at the time of the presentation, thereby transforming the lecture-oriented meeting into one in which everyone is encouraged to participate.

It has thus become ordinary for any project or activity— from project specifications to presentation to the managing directors—requiring the intervention of several participants to be accompanied by visual presentations. As many professionals have observed, in the specific framework of the conduct of a meeting, this practice has numerous advantages, if only in terms of speed of execution and the fact that a single medium is used: the same medium can serve as the agenda, the table of contents, a supplement to the oral presentation, a transcript, and even an official act and reference document.

The last type, the *communication meeting* (events, performances, shows), represents in a sense the quintessence of the genus, exemplified by presentations of results at annual shareholders' meetings. In this case, the usual arrangement is a lecture format: a single speaker, standing, walking, or stationary behind a rostrum, who speaks, shows his slides, stimulates, and acts like a master of ceremonies. He carries the presentation entirely; he may be its designer, the person in charge, or simply its interpreter. He directs discussion. This very professorial arrangement has enabled PowerPoint to make its way in many academic settings: lecture, dissertation defense, speech, sermon, and so on.

So a PowerPoint presentation requires real skill in group stimulation and a certain capacity to control interactions. Not everyone can be a group leader. Although for a teacher, politician, lawyer, preacher, or actor, speaking in public does not pose any particular problem, either because of innate talent or because of an expensive coach, for ordinary people the exercise is often a painful ordeal. For that reason, in the context of work relations requiring this kind of public speaking with increasing frequency, it is hardly surprising that training sessions on the conduct of meetings have exploded in companies and administrations. Mastery of the technique of running a meeting has become one of the indispensable skills for any manager who wants to advance: today it is a good idea to be demonstrative and a good actor if one wants to have a career in business.

The position of presenter is never an easy one. As in any relationship involving communication, rapport with the audience must be established. The exercise is not free of risk for the presenter, who is often staking the legitimacy of his status or his job; he stages himself and subjects himself to an implicit evaluation by his peers and/or his superiors of his competence, his skill, and, more seriously, of his self-presentation, his behavior. As Gérald Gaglio has noted, a presentation "is a risky scene. The actor has to control his own face and that of a group (his 'institute,' his team), carry out a presentation of himself in which his reputation is at stake. For this reason, presenters have 'good reasons' to learn in depth how to use the technical device studied because that prevents unpleasant surprises in the dangerous interaction represented by the meeting and its many purposes, which are often ambiguous."[3]

Indeed, in a PowerPoint presentation, the speaker is the only living focus of attention. He is a valued actor who has the power of speech and the ability to lead the discussion, but at the same time, he is in competition with the presentation itself (the slides), because the audience alternates its attention between him and the screen.

This situation has several consequences. There is, to begin with, a risk that attention will be diluted. The audience also may choose to navigate through the presentation according to its own interests or to do something entirely different. The projected text, for example, makes it possible to select the important points without having to listen to the speaker. This fragmentation, this dispersal of tasks, according to some sociologists of work, is one of the major pathologies in the contemporary workplace, multitasking.[4]

An American study states that PowerPoint presentations are often "corporate sleeping pills,"[5] and meetings with PowerPoint are sites of boredom. As the presenter is still explaining the first point on his slide, the audience has already gone through the entire thing. The author asserts that 73 percent of attendees bring other work to these meetings. And Valérie Beaudoin comments, "Presentations, especially when they are long, deaden the audience's capacity to respond."[6]

Whereas a meeting is intended to be a site for exchanges, the mediation provided by PowerPoint creates hypnotic effects that make the audience totally inert. And in a vicious circle, the more inert the audience, the more the presenter has to struggle to catch its constantly distracted attention. This is a diabolical logic according to which "value resides in the ability to capture the attention of the other, which means one is entering into an economy of attention in which value is created by seizing the other's time."[7]

A second effect is the logic of evaluation that a PowerPoint presentation puts into operation. An engineer from France Telecom, for instance, tells of project reviews in which an employee is forced to defend each of his slides in front of a dozen co-workers involved in the same project, who are therefore theoretically united in solidarity: "You start to pick up the slightest snigger, you are hurt by the slightest criticism, the smallest counter-argument. The solemn and spectacular aspect of the presentation accentuates the sense of being on trial. I think work meetings have become tenser because this staging necessarily produces increased stress beyond the conduct of the project itself, which is already rather complex."

These presentation sessions sometimes become a war of all against all in which everyone tries to seize center stage and establish power. Although these are fairly common aspects of group dynamics, the sense of exhibition, performance, and even competition among individuals—aggravated by the narcissism of some of them—accentuates the contrast between the success of some presentations and the failure of others.

According to Cécile Tardy, Yves Jeanneret, and Julien Hamard, the PowerPoint format provides speakers with four performance choices: In *speech governed by writing*, the speaker has no latitude and follows exactly what is written on the screen. This is the "prompter" format, which provokes the greatest number of criticisms. In *semi-improvised speech*, the speaker goes back and forth between screen and audience. The speaker's body is freer (in profile between audience and screen). If the speaker departs too far from his presentation, however, the public may tune out, not knowing whether it is supposed to read or listen. In *speech as spectacle*, the projected image and text become a support, highlighting a statement like the caption of a photograph. Speech becomes theatrical and hypnotic, intended to charm. Less often, in *disjointed speech*, there can be a gap between what is said and the document presented. This is often the case if nothing is projected and the slide is a document providing for interaction. Some firms systematically offer this kind of document, closer to a report than a presentation.[8]

In the spectacle, the speaker and her speech, gestures, and messages are no longer the only focus of the audience's attention—and therein lies one of PowerPoint's strengths and its major weakness. Visual presentation offers the audience a multiplicity of distractions: reading of the slides alone, paying attention to the back-and-forth between speaker and screen, listening to the speaker alone, shifting between speaker and slides, talking with neighbors, taking notes, and so on: "A presenter can easily disappear behind his presentation and stop being responsible for it. . . . Insofar as the slide show has been prepared by others, all that remains is an ego in charge, who is disengaged."[9]

Although PowerPoint facilitates the organization of the per-formance, it also tends to oblige the presenter to capture his audience's attention, particularly by carefully aligning what he says with what he projects: "The presenter has to coordinate the flow of words, which is continuous by nature, with the proces-sion of slide images in which the text is presented in blocks. It is not a simple matter to reconcile the continuous and the discon-tinuous, and as soon as technology gets involved, the speaker re-acts. . . . In 'good' presentations, the speaker is not content with ensuring there is a threefold alignment (among what he says, what is projected, and his audience) with his eyes. He mobilizes his body to continuously recreate links between the screen, his words, and the audience."[10]

Although, in the confined setting of a meeting room, capti-vating a dozen colleagues with the validity of a new computer application or a new purchasing system is not the essential purpose—the issue is rather to make decisions—it is nonetheless the case that the work meeting has become, thanks to or because of the required use of PowerPoint, a performance in the sense of an exhibition. The injunction to communicate and techno-logical sophistication have created an inflated spectacle, trans-forming the slightest briefing into a show. Not only does the software distort the meeting but it also imposes unprecedented constraints. It is no longer the content that creates its own rules of exposition, but the technical medium.

The German sociologist Hubert Knoblauch has demon-strated the capacity of the tool to turn a simple presentation into a performance,[11] more specifically what he defines as "the performance of knowledge." Through the use of the pointer, the speaker assigns knowledge a position in space. Instead of translating, explaining, and teaching a fact or circumstance, the knowledge to be shared in a presentation is defined by the way it is represented in space with speech, movement, and image. The audience thus faces "presented knowledge" and staging rather than a sharing or transmission of knowledge.[12] What is involved is giving something to be seen, not giving something to be known, and above all showing that the presenter has mastered the knowledge that he is showing the audience. Hence the talent of consultants is to know how to stage their expertise so they can later sell it.[13]

PROMOTIONAL PERFORMANCE

The widespread use of PowerPoint in meetings has modified the way in which information is shared and discussed. Many meetings have become pure exhibitions, particularly in a professional sector where the aim is to be seen and to use charm to make the audience buy: the world of marketing and advertising.

The vogue of marketing goes back to the 1950s. In the postwar economic boom, under the reign of the media, mass consumption, and more intense competition, companies began to become interested in consumers: they sensed it was time to pay a little more attention to the people at the end point of their production chain, the customers.

Marketing and public relations employees were quick to adopt PowerPoint: all the graphic designers of the 1990s worked on Macintoshes, and computer culture and graphics tools spread rapidly in public relations circles and beyond. Companies, relying increasingly on public relations departments, eagerly adopted these new technological tools. Along with Photoshop/Illustrator, FrontPage/Dreamweaver, Xpress, and Flash,[14] the basic toolbox for any self-respecting graphic designer and advertiser, the Office suite, particularly PowerPoint, has become indispensable for the business.

The purpose of promotional language is to make available in a consensual way, with warmth and closeness, information that is in principle reliable and likely to trigger a purchase. Whether for reconstructing studies, focus group responses, or the results of consumer surveys or for presentations, briefings, advertising campaign proposals, promotional events, or sponsoring, the advantage of PowerPoint lies in the fact that it can quickly and easily be made into a medium for everything at once: demonstration, reconstruction, summary report, and finally staging of a performance intended to charm for the purpose of selling a service, generally a public relations program or a major advertising campaign worth several million euros.

A research director for an institute, Anne-Sophie O., runs focus groups and meetings of consumers. She writes her analyses and reports directly in PowerPoint out of a concern for efficiency, because the report is presented orally and writing directly in PowerPoint enables her to have a simpler style with briefer expressions. Anne-Sophie belongs to the new generation of consultants; that is, she came to the profession after PowerPoint was already its primary tool.

A brand specialist, Cesare P., a semiologist of Italian origin, adopted PowerPoint both because of market constraint and for personal convenience. But he remains very critical: "With the computer, we produced longer and longer reports, at least fifty slides. On each slide, you have to put images, graphs, tables. You have to work faster and faster. Time that used to be spent thinking and writing fairly well-constructed pages I now spend looking for images and formatting them. Clients look to see above all whether the slides look good: if they're pretty, it's a good study. Our audiences flip through our work as though it was a magazine. Besides, our studies are written as though they were magazines."

Another experienced employee, Bruno R., is also familiar with this evolution from the written to the projected and the constraints of presentation: "I immediately found it very restrictive. First because you have to follow a thread. Then, because you can't play around with the time for the presentation. You are always late in relation to the time set by the presentation itself. Obviously, you can 'freeze' a slide, or change it, make it evolve. But in general, since you never know in advance what you will talk about in greater depth, it is very delicate. You end up eliminating very interesting things, the only way to catch up with the time you've lost, or you run through important elements at great speed." According to him, the rigidity of PowerPoint means that it is impossible to skip elements without that being obvious. The software permits neither accident nor fantasy. And whenever someone asks a question, there is the danger of a digression, and the presentation then becomes completely chaotic.

PowerPoint is a medium for the instantaneous; it is truncated, too brief; it does not allow for the persistent association of ideas provided by linear reading. It is a restrained, limited medium, because it is designed solely so that a certain quantity of content can enter into a frame and become visible. Bruno observes bitterly: "We sell time—the time we save our clients—and not scientific research. The slides themselves decide what is important or secondary; they themselves make the choice."

For these experts in manipulating signs and images, these advertisers and public relations people, the influence of the medium, the domination of the frame, and the attraction for the immediate and quickly digestible visual contain both obvious qualities and real dangers. But all recognize that it is now hardly possible to do without PowerPoint. In every response to a call for proposals, the competitors are forced to design a recommendation that is glamorous and dynamic, organized around a few focal points, while providing a very well-constructed technical response, often in the form of a thick "academic" document.

Very carefully designed slides intended for a high-class oral presentation—we are among public relations professionals—these PowerPoint presentations are also highly technical working documents forced to follow the rules imposed by the software. There is no way advertisers or any business hero can get around this new ambiguity of the medium, except by concentration on the spectacular side of the presentation. And some champion presenters have grasped this fact.

PERFORMANCE BUSINESS

Over the course of a few years, the late head of Apple became a past master in the realm of spectacle, to the point that entire books have been written about his talents as a presenter.

Steve Jobs's shows began on January 24, 1984, for the release of the first Macintosh. It is touching today to see the young man in a black suit with a bow tie, a little ironic smile at the corner of his mouth as though he'd just made a bad joke, presenting the machine that revolutionized the computer market. Obviously, presentations at the time did not yet use dedicated software. But the procedure was already well honed. Even though Jobs, just out of his garage with Steve Wozniak, read his notes, spoke too fast, and stood awkwardly, he made a few jokes, manipulated projected photographs, and played with numbers.

All the ingredients were present. And Steve Jobs had a great sense of drama. One of the main arguments for the advantage of Macintosh over the large systems of the time was its size and

portability. In the midst of his presentation, like a stage magician, Jobs opens a bag and takes out a Mac. Then he puts it on
the rostrum, turns it on, and its name appears on the screen:
Macintosh. The computer is the star of the presentation. The
lights go out, mysterious music is heard—*Tubular Bells* by Mike
Oldfield[15]—and all the machine's features start to parade on the
screen, crowning the show.

This type of exhibition symbolizes one of Apple's trademarks.
Every year since 1984, the manufacturer has organized a large
conference to which it invites the "Apple family." The California
company understood early the marketing value of creating a
community of users, as opposed to mere consumers. The most
famous of these gatherings is the Macworld Conference Expo
that takes place in January every year. Apple presents its earnings, its plans, and its new software and hardware. The "Mac
family" waits like impatient fans for Steve Notes, the boss's presentation.[16] Over the years, these annual meetings have become
highly codified ceremonies, the staging of which Steve Jobs has
brought to a high polish. Helped by increasingly inventive technology, the entertainer of the early days turned into a guru able
to convert millions of the faithful into purchasers of his latest
technological gadgets.

Boston, January 1997, Macworld Conference Expo: it is a historic moment. As the mythical brand is running out of steam—
not only are the numbers down, but the notoriety and the
originality of Apple are under severe strain—Steve Jobs, then
president of Pixar,[17] returns after ten years away. He is greeted
like a messiah by the Apple community, which sees his return as
a sign of renewal. The company needs shock treatment, and only
"papa" can cure the child.

The show meets expectations in Hollywood style. Flanked by
two large kakemonos with Apple insignia, the stage is huge and

the screen monumental. In contrast, the speaker and the rostrum seem minute. This stage effect allows the public to fix its attention simultaneously on the performer and the screen and makes it possible to alternate between close-ups and wide shots. A warm-up speaker presents the company's numbers and press reports from recent months. The tension gradually rises, as in a rock concert. Murmuring, glances to the left, he's coming, here he is, the "supreme guide" is back, Steve Jobs is back in business. First standing ovation.

The presentation follows a well-tried plan: brief slide on earnings—better to be quick; they're bad—then Steve Jobs, armed with his remote, the essential tool of Steve Notes, briefly recounts his time at Pixar, then follows with three quotations that appear on the screen.

"Apple has become irrelevant."

"Apple can't execute anything."[18]

"Apple's culture is anarchy; you can't manage it."

Jobs's entire presentation is based on these three negative judgments. The procedure is clever; it enables him to build, practically in real time, Apple's new strategy on the basis of criticisms made of it and to bring out the value of the innovative products and services intended to contradict these received ideas.

Jobs's first trick is to rely on the audience's taste for numbers. The use of a number as image or emblem is an indication of his way of using a mere item of management information as an element of communication: quantity thus becomes a sign of quality.[19] The number of units sold, hard-drive capacity, prices, market share—all become icons of Apple's success over the years, powerful elements of memory. After tables and graphs, Jobs is content to project just one number per slide, a kind of abstraction of number, to produce a shock effect.

One of the first climaxes in the show is the presentation of the new management team. After a Hollywood-style display—photographs of the candidates and their titles (all heavyweights of American business, including the co-founder of Oracle, Larry Ellison)—Jobs shows a video in which each member of the board gives his sense of the company's future, in the form of a documentary interview.

Rather than a usual lineup on the stage, a fake roundtable with a moderator or a beauty-pageant-style parade, Jobs opts for high-tech staging, bringing out the ubiquity of the tool and especially its great possibilities. Exhibiting technology in this way has a twofold advantage: it is useful for staging, and it heightens the value of the product. In addition, this mastery is accented by Steve Jobs in the role of demiurge, directing each element of the spectacle with his remote, which he uses like a magic wand with authority and precision.

After the film, the speaker takes the floor again, using another basic tool of presentation: interaction with the public, usually in the form of questions and answers. What are Apple's main strengths? "Its 25 million worldwide users, meaning you!" Another ovation. The audience is happy; it has become the hero of the presentation. Being able to connect with the audience is one of the keys to a successful PowerPoint presentation. Steve Jobs goes further, seeking complicity, connivance, even identification.

A skillful stage manager, the head of Apple creates a new surprise. After playing around with the names of operating systems: Tempo, Allegro, and Requiem, alluding to the firm's sad financial state, he commits the irreparable by bringing the fox into the henhouse—the sworn enemy, Bill Gates, the boss of Microsoft, creator of Windows and copier of Apple.[20] It seems implausible. And yet Bill Gates appears on the giant screen and states that he has agreed to sign an armistice. Despite a few boos in the room, this staging made possible through technology ends one of Jobs's most celebrated conferences. The boss was once again able to create a sensation, a moment that everyone in the community and beyond will remember. And this was done through the artifice of a videoconference, a performance in the performance. The content of the agreement with Bill Gates hardly mattered; the main thing was its staging and the image of Gates and Jobs congratulating each other: virtually signing a contract at a distance and live, thanks to the miracles of technology, made for a magnificent spectacle. Apple had entered into a new age of conquest.

Then there was MacWorld 2007. Thinner, the irresistible salesman did not hesitate as soon as he stepped onstage to announce that Apple was in the process of writing a new chapter in its history and in history in general. This show came at the end of ten years of practice giving presentations and, particularly because of technological developments, showcased all the rhetorical effects made possible by the tool and the speaker's talent. But the setup had hardly changed. After a musical introduction—"I Feel Good," by James Brown, rather mischievous at a time when Jobs's health was in question—the boss of Apple began the litany of events and earnings for the company over the year just ended. The performance was the pretext for an exuberant display of devices polished over the years: quotations,[21] incessant slogans,[22] hyperbolic language, and the power of numbers: all the ingredients were thrown together.

When he announced the creation of his television network, Jobs came to the show's first climax. The "family" was waiting impatiently for the birth of the latest offspring.[23] "You're going to experience a historic moment that you go through only once in a lifetime." By putting together the wizardry of the iPod and a large touch screen, a revolutionary telephone and unprecedented

Internet access, "Apple has reinvented the telephone." As an experienced performer, Jobs played with three projected images and with his voice repeating "iPod" and "Phone" in rapid succession to produce his new gadget, the iPhone. It was a triumph of multimedia theatricality. The description of the product drew on all the resources of imagery: a comical photographic montage of a cobbled-together mobile phone alluding to "business school" competitors as Jobs commented ironically, easy effects concluding with another theatrical gesture. One of the iPhone's great innovations was its interface, the finger. And he joked "All finger gestures are allowed."

Steve Jobs then used a new artifice made possible by the technology, using the medium to stage himself, not just the product. The arrangement was fairly simple: the iPhone was displayed on the giant screen, and in a window was Steve Jobs's hand holding the device, filmed by a mini-camera. The display on the screen and the live manipulation in the theater were completely synchronous, as though Jobs were producing the screen display then and there (one even had a moment of doubt). The magical character of the demonstration and the complete mastery of communication maintained the illusion. The effect spoke for itself, and the spectator was more dazzled by the performance and the spectacle than by the product being offered, its functionalities, its design, its simplicity.

Carmine Gallo, a communications expert, came up with the idea of dissecting, analyzing, and commenting on hours and hours of Jobs's presentations, from which he constructed a handbook: *The Presentation Secrets of Steve Jobs: How to Be Insanely Great in Front of Any Audience*. Writing in *Businessweek* in October 2009, Gallo described the Jobs conference as the return of the greatest storyteller in the world: "Steve Jobs does not sell computers; he sells an experience. The same holds true for his presentations that are meant to inform, educate, and entertain. An Apple presentation has all the elements of a great theatrical production—a great script, heroes and villains, stage props, breathtaking visuals, and one moment that makes the price of admission well worth it."

For Gallo, Jobs's presentations provide a sort of apprenticeship for presentation, a pedagogy in action. Aside from the usual tricks of a good PowerPoint presentation—simple slides, well organized argument, speaker involvement, moments of feeling, and so on—he points to some unusual innovations that make Steve Jobs a great stage director: constant invention of an enemy against which Apple must always fight,[24] an extraordinary feeling for slogans, the ability to make sense out of numbers by magnifying them, and a constant search for analogies or comparisons to make them as eloquent as possible. And finally, Steve Jobs has the ability to create memorable moments, discreetly accentuated by technological wizardry, that the audience will long remember.

With Steve Jobs, we touch on the quintessence of oral presentation. The performance becomes its own subject, the medium mediates itself and is no longer there simply to communicate messages and persuade an audience. Through an excess of charm, the presentation becomes self-creating, self-promoting, and self-absorbed.

POLITICAL PERFORMANCE

It is therefore hardly surprising that staging itself is staged and that the presentation itself becomes the subject, for example, of a movie script.

An Inconvenient Truth, directed by Davis Guggenheim and starring former Vice President Al Gore, was one of the most successful American documentaries in recent years. It is a ninety-four-minute film that relies on a multimedia presentation prepared by the 2007 Nobel Peace Prize winner[25] in the context of a campaign to increase awareness of climate change in cities around the world.

Shown at the Sundance Film Festival in 2006[26] and later at the Cannes Festival, the film won two Oscars in 2007 (best documentary and best original song). Who would have thought that a film whose pitch might have been: "It's a movie about global warming, starring Al Gore, doing a slide show, with charts,"[27] would become such a worldwide success: $23 million in ticket sales in the United States and more than six hundred thousand tickets sold in France?

Following an unprecedented model, *An Inconvenient Truth* relies on a slide presentation that alternates informative sequences of images, videos, and commentaries with more militant passages from the speaker, sprinkled with stories of the hero's personal life. Rather than simply dryly and mechanically enumerating facts, the film plays both on emotion and on the scientific character of its argument. The staging oscillates between an "objective" presentation of facts and data, certified by the projection of slides, and a manifest temptation to dramatize the argument with many incidents and anecdotes.

This impression was confirmed by the director, Davis Guggenheim: When "the producers came to me," he said in an interview, "I said to them directly I don't know if you can make a movie about a slide show." He went to a presentation and was "blown away." "I left after an hour and a half thinking that global warming was the most important issue. . . . I had no idea how you'd make a film out of it, but I wanted to try."[28] With the help of the constant alternation between narrative and scientific

exposition, Davis Guggenheim won his bet and made a successful movie out of a slide show.

From the very beginning of the film, the staging—recalling
Apple's Steve Notes—is in place and leaves no doubt about the
kind of show the audience will see: a theater, auditorium, am-
phitheater, or lecture hall, in any event a spacious site suggesting the idea of a performance; a narrow rostrum on which is a
Macintosh portable computer and a remote; and plasma screens
placed around the stage. The relaxed lecturer-actor Al Gore is
tieless and moves around freely: the posture resonates in relation to his status as a statesman and gives a less institutional and
more relaxed flavor to his argument. Finally, there is the palpable
presence of the audience, which seems to have already been won
over by the speaker's status, by the theme of civic responsibility,
by other audience members, and by the images projected on a
large screen behind Gore.

To dissipate any ambiguity about one of Al Gore's primary
sources of inspiration, the camera often focuses on the logo of
his portable computer, the celebrated apple. The former vice
president has indeed made himself into a modern figure of an
ecologist permanently connected to the world's networks, in
touch with current news and scientific and political developments, a reputation confirmed in several of the film's scenes
where he is seen constantly working at his microphone, reading
the newspapers, consulting documents, watching videos, preparing speeches, and exchanging e-mails.

A promoter of "information highways" in the Clinton administration, Al Gore did in fact play an important role in the development of the Internet and new information technologies. His
relationship with Apple is so solid that he became a board member in 2003. After failing to persuade Congress to sign the Kyoto
Protocol in 1997 and after his defeat by George W. Bush in the

2000 presidential elections, Gore started giving multimedia lectures on global warming around the world. The film shows us the PowerPoint presentation in the process of being developed, a veritable practical handbook for using the software: the former vice president develops his slide show, arranges his graphs and charts, and tweaks his staging event after event, in front of small or large audiences. Gore presented the various versions of this slide show at least a thousand times between 2000 and 2004.

Several times in the film, he plays around with his own role as an American hero, skillfully mixing biographical and historical anecdotes: election defeat, his son's accident, life with his parents, and the emotional account of his sister Nancy's cancer, which led to his giving up his father's tobacco farm. These biographical details make up a "mythical" tale intercut with photographs of glaciers, floods, hurricanes, and uncluttered graphs in which temperature curves or CO_2 levels appear in red or blue.

The film opens with a few luxuriant images of the planet taken from satellite photographs. Splendid images and the "family romance"—the former political star has found the right method: "I want to show you this because I want to tell you a story." The public is reassured: it is not going to hear a boring lecture. But the story has to be educational: they are also there to learn something. Al Gore mentions one of his teachers, Roger Revelle, a figure around whom he builds the fable of the old master who has understood everything and enlightens the young hero. The presentation device is ideal for this emotional slide show, with photographs of the professor in his classroom, presenting his graphs, his tables of numbers, and his diagrams. We are somewhere between hagiography and a scientific account, where emotion shares the stage with professorial authority and legend with scientific expertise. We are in the register of narrative (the biography of a hero, the scientist, recounted by another hero, the politician) built on a scientific discourse and its accessories (numbers, graphs, and the like) which also provides a kind of show within the show that the audience is attending,

We have barely left Revelle's blackboard when we are face-to-face with the snows of Kilimanjaro that are disappearing year after year. The presentation moves back and forth between a tone of militancy and a more didactic style. Either it is a course in a scholarly atmosphere where there is pleasure in learning or, as in China, our hero asserts with heartfelt conviction, "We have to separate truth from fiction."

The impact of the techniques is multiplied by the cinematic effects. Al Gore does not hesitate to pull out all the stops. For example, there is an elevator onstage that enables him to rise nine feet in the air to show the audience the dizzying rise in CO_2 levels in coming years. The hyperbolic effects are further accentuated: language, numbers, graphs, gestures, staging. All the accessories are magnified by camera angles. Every shot can be systematically given emphasis through graphic effects to mark the spectator's memory. The doubly fixed image—in the presentation and in the film—creates a mesmerizing sensation.

For example, to bring out the ten years when temperatures on the planet were the highest, Gore creates an animation on a timeline to have them appear gradually. For the 2003 heat wave, temperature numbers associated with the number of deaths recorded in the form of bullet lists are distributed on maps. Then beautiful photographs of hurricanes are projected with their nicknames, followed by a stack of images, like an iconographic list, illustrating phenomena as different as the melting of glaciers, the appearance of new diseases, the study of bleached corals, or the observation of migratory birds in Holland, alternating with curves, diagrams, and 3-D animations. This inflation of techniques stuns the dual spectator—of the presentation and of the film—who has to make the distinction between multiform, hypertrophied, and confused information and the persuasive arguments of the principal actor.

To create a break, a climax that might wake the audience from the narcotic effect produced by the torrent of images and information, Al Gore uses a rather rudimentary device, an argument from authority directly derived from PowerPoint thinking: a full-screen display of a quotation. One example among others: "The era of procrastination, of half-measures, of soothing and baffling expedients, of delays, is coming to its close. In its place we are entering a period of consequences." The statement is taken from a speech given by Winston Churchill in the House of Commons on November 12, 1936, following German occupation of the Rhineland. Incidentally, this quotation, frequently used in different contexts, particularly by some management consultants, has become a real gimmick in PowerPoint presentations.[29] The extent to which excess amplification and a taste for the spectacular can lead to manipulation and deliberate confusion is clear, in this case between the prelude to World War II and the ecological problems of the early twenty-first century.

PowerPoint thinking makes itself evident also in its ability to dramatize numbers. In order to show the exponential increase in damages from natural disasters, Gore does not turn to spectacular and terrifying images of flooding in Bangladesh; he presents a bar graph from insurance companies and a bullet list of data and numbers. The paradox of the PowerPoint show is that tragedy is made more distant, but numbers and letters make the tragedy more rational. Al Gore has learned from Steve Jobs how to give meaning to a number that then becomes the source of a dramatic effect: 37 inches of water in 24 hours, a water level reaching 7 feet, the most rain a city has had in one day, 1,000 dead. The number operates as a sign with extra emotional value, stronger than an image. It also makes it possible to bring out a piece of information from an uninterrupted flow of composite images: a single number or a single word is sometimes more valuable than even a suggestive image.

The technique on which the film is based, the PowerPoint slide, is ubiquitous, even when it serves no purpose: in the film, whenever Gore speaks as a narrator outside the setting of a lecture, he still uses slides or shows himself preparing slides, as though we were in his studio watching the story being made, like documentaries on rock group tours.

The presentation is therefore not only a medium for speech and an accessory of the show; it is itself the subject of the show. The film follows the format of the lecture, and it is the form of the slide show that designs and structures the messages. Meaning comes not from the presenter, the speech, or the images, but from the interaction of these three elements and their narrative progression, which establishes an attractive staging.

A "PERFORMANCE OF KNOWLEDGE"

Advertising, business, and political show are all uses of Power-Point presentations that demonstrate the plasticity of a device used as much as an advanced prompter as a scientific alibi or a dramaturgical accessory. The millions of presentations made around the world every day fail, of course, to match the star models. But as the saying goes, If you can do the hard part, the rest is easy. The most troubling thing is that this form of "digital rhetoric" is used in every sector of activity.

To bring out the new forms of the language of political argument in the era of digital media, the sociologists David Stark and Verena Paravel point to the example of the reception given the seven architects' proposals for the reconstruction of the World

Trade Center. And they demonstrate how, thanks to the variety of media at its disposal, PowerPoint can present stories overflowing with emotion designed to win over a jury judging the proposals:

> All the architects' presentations were stories of remembrance, reconciliation, and renaissance; all were dedicated to making a resurrected global city. Their task of representing rebirth was facilitated by one of the most powerful affordances of PowerPoint technology. Thanks to the *exact over-impression* of slides and the skill with which they paced it, architects could produce the feeling that, from a monumentally tragic occurrence, a life-affirming opportunity could emerge.[30]

Stark and Paravel note that all the competing firms worked with the effects made possible by the software to animate, make their presentations "alive" and dynamic, particularly the technique of over-impression, which brings life out of a field of ruins, something that would be totally impossible with flip charts: "Technical function meets rhetorical purpose with persuasive effect." PowerPoint does not show two images, a before and an after; it stages the rebirth. It makes it possible to show the progress of the project and the living character of the process. The architects were faced with a challenge, because they had to show the monumental character of the project while simultaneously establishing close contact with the audience. Aside from the usual commonplaces (such as photographs of mothers and children), the presenters relied on cinematic effects like the alternation between wide and tight views, between close-ups and tracking shots. Finally, 3-D images allowed the audience to enter the building.

In this performance context, it is worth considering the

interaction among the presenter, his projection, the accessories, and the audience. Analyzing the stage performance and particularly the role of the pointer in a certain number of presentations, Knoblauch, as we have seen, defines the PowerPoint presentation as a "performance of knowledge."[31] The technological relationship adds a supplemental mediation to the traditional lecture format, turning it into a hybrid, representative of what the information (or knowledge) society now produces. It is a hybrid insofar as this type of performance borrows from the scientific and academic spheres while using registers taken from management practices: "Although visual media in lectures had long been common in education and the scientific world, the increasing technical sophistication of visual presentation has recently been stimulated by public relations and management."[32]

This combination of genres, where form often dominates content, poses a problem of which the PowerPoint performance is a symptom:

> The proliferation of PowerPoint exemplifies a form of de-specialization and dissolution of the social and institutional boundaries of knowledge that characterizes any communication transmitted by computer, internet, or e-mail. The fact that the same form of communication can be used in different types of institutional presentations demonstrates the increasing resemblance of the kinds knowledge transmitted in these forms. The dissolution of the boundaries of knowledge existing until now has become visible, because, whatever the knowledge dispensed by PowerPoint, the form is not affected. In all examples, this transmission of knowledge depends on the fact that it is performed. The reasons for this performance of knowledge can be found in the very functioning that contributes to its success: the dissolution of the institutional boundaries of knowledge (that is,

knowledge organized by discipline or profession) and, even more the progression of the de-institutionalization and decontextualization of the communication of knowledge through technological media. . . . The performance is, so to speak, a work of repair designed to standardize processes of communication in a *knowledge society* that depends more and more on that knowledge to function.[33]

The PowerPoint performance pursues very precise goals and adopts various strategies for that purpose. For example, there is the business that "sells" only standardized models of knowledge and encourages a style of showmanship and theatricality. In the political realm, there is the intention to persuade and make decisions, always with a touch of the documentary, of "reality," intended to make its dramaturgy more persuasive.

With its kind of ordinary and utilitarian knowledge, Power-Point content has to take on an "original" form and present an "original" performance to obscure the poverty of its argument. As a performance device, PowerPoint stages its own capacity to manipulate basic knowledge by merely exhibiting it. This standardized performance does not allow the spectators to discuss or contradict. A major tool of the knowledge society, PowerPoint does not live from that knowledge but from its exhibition alone. Knowledge doesn't matter; it's enough to show that you know.

6

THE POWER OF CONSULTANTS

➡

An archetypal scene of social life in the early twenty-first century: four shadowy figures emerge from an ill-lit corridor: a woman of about thirty, well dressed but not flashy, with glasses, her blond hair in a bob; two young men dressed in identical dark gray suits with narrow trousers that are a little too short, wide ties with bright colors, a white or sky blue fitted shirt, that touch of elegance that distinguishes them from vulgar salesmen, carrying attaché cases and spiral-bound notebooks; and finally an older man who is very elegant, smiling, with a detached air. The two young men set up their laptops, apparently calm; they all have one except for the man who looks like the boss.

After pleasantries and the exchange of business cards, the installation begins with the connection of a laptop to a video projector. A slight hesitation for both performers and audience: "Where is the outlet? Thank you. Where is the screen? Very good. Can we start? Go ahead." The room usually goes dark, the title slide with a logo appears, and the ceremony can begin.

This ritual occurs millions of times a year, in offices, rooms, and amphitheaters everywhere in the world, with the same rules, the same form, the same language, the same accessories. How did this means of communication spread so widely and take on such importance in the lives of millions of individuals around the world? Who today could contemplate organizing a meeting of any importance without access to a PowerPoint projection?

It has to be acknowledged that this practice has grown considerably in just twenty years thanks to the continuing invasion of armies of consultants in every corner of private and public enterprises. It is a regular and permanent occupation intended to spread their good methods, their perceptive analyses, their organizational methods, their strategic recommendations—in short, models of thinking concocted in managerial agencies primarily based in the United States.

This democratization and proliferation of new models of thinking surfaced in the early 1980s after various economic disturbances, particularly the two oil shocks. Companies at the time were forced to substantially change their organizational and operational methods. They had to resolve to take the medication prescribed by the only "therapists" able to treat them—consultants, strategic advisers serving many companies in public relations and information systems.[1]

Thanks to the thousands of person-days sold to client companies and the millions of slides repeating essentially the same models and the same arguments, these experts in recommendations have been able to link rationality, authority, and entertainment, if not to help their clients, at least to enrich their employers.

Where do these consultants come from? What models do they sell through their presentations? How do they put them together? These are some of the questions addressed in this chapter.

MANAGING ORGANIZATIONS: A JOB FOR ENGINEERS

From the beginning, management has been the prerogative of scientists and, in industry, the army, or transportation, often of engineers. Even if their status varies around the world—the profession of engineer has a unique character in France[2]—it must be acknowledged that the gurus of the organization of work frequently come from scientific and technical backgrounds, like Frederick W. Taylor, Henry Ford, Alfred Sloan, Henri Fayol, Octave Gélinier, John Kotter, and Henry Mintzberg. It is hardly surprising that implementing increasingly complex organizations by putting together skills both technical and financial requires the intervention of scientific experts and their box of tools. Consultants and engineers also have an inherent propensity to formalize and standardize practices that frequently involves simplification.

A large number of consultants were weaned on organizational models devised in the early twentieth century by engineers, such as the American Frederick W. Taylor or the Frenchman Henri Fayol, whose models are based on a few simple principles. From the "scientific organization of work" to "goal management," "operational research," and "strategic management," the entire history of management consists of meeting three principles: ensuring control over and mastery of an organization, being efficient and effective, and adopting a methodical and rational approach to problems—"*Mastery, Results, and Rationality* make up the management logo of the company."[3]

Patrick M. worked for fifteen years at Accenture as a computer engineering consultant. Like many consultants, he was trained as an engineer and thus learned to use engineering tools, such as modeling. He justifies the procedure this way:

Like every engineer, I already have a "natural" approach—through experience and intellectual training—to modeling. A consultant who wants to get messages across doesn't write a twenty-page document, but draws a picture or makes a graph. The consultant is trying to get his ideas across, and the best way to do that without taking too much time is to quickly formalize his thinking, simplify it, even "caricature" it; it's efficient because it's more readable for the client. Formalization and simplification facilitate the expression of ideas.

This testimony is confirmed by Olivier Babeau, a professor of management: "The preponderance of those trained as engineers in [consulting] firms is explained by the special value attributed to mathematical ability. The ability to formalize is an essential component of a consultant's expertise. It is by integrating this formalization into a summary presentation that he can produce the illuminating slides the clients expect."[4]

The value of modeling lies in its simplifying and reassuring effects. What is a model? A representation of a concrete or real system by a formal object which makes it possible to think about the system but also to act on it. The three essential characteristics are: (1) its reductionism (only a few characteristics of the real system are contained in the model); (2) its bias (the representation is oriented by the tools of observation and of theoretical thinking, but also by the goals of the modeler); and (3) its reversibility: the model is both an abstraction of a preexisting reality and a prototype or basis for a future construction, original or copy, archetype or realization.[5]

The analogy with the guiding principles of PowerPoint is striking. *Reductionism* echoes the principles of simplification, summarizing, and reduction that govern every PowerPoint presentation. *Bias* evokes the designer's ability to produce a performance designed to capture the audience. *Reversibility* expresses the ability to produce an object on the basis of an observation—every study begins with an "audit"—and then to transform it into a practical recipe that one copies and pastes and applies endlessly.

With the rise of computer technology and military research, modeling based on mathematical formalization increased, particularly in economics, fostering the birth of a new discipline, econometrics.[6] Even then, some researchers expressed reservations about models created for the army being adopted for the economy. And indeed, the tendency to extend military-inspired models to other spheres of activity only grew worse over time.

These models play an important role, for example, in polls and politicians' choices in the United States and other developed countries. These techniques—grouped under the heading of "operational research"[7]—are applied not only to macroeconomic policies but to everything related to the organization, management, and rationalization of human activity. These practices again originated in the military: any action in the theater of operations requires planning and the coordination of various resources.

With the emergence of game theory in the 1950s, the galaxy of mathematical and economic models were closely intertwined in pursuit of the goals of optimizing the choices of users of public services, as well as for traders, lawyers, or military leaders. In addition, the expansionism of the new informational and cybernetic language had perceptible influence on modes of representation. By the 1950s, it was hard to conceal the inputs, outputs, and feedbacks, as well as all the categories of graphs, diagrams, and charts of all sorts called on to illustrate with simplicity and artistic sense often complex and difficult subjects.

Computer science, its materials, tools, and language, gained an influence in the 1970s, that has persisted up to the present.[8] So much so that computer engineers have gradually become the real bosses of some companies, particularly in the service sector (banks and insurance companies). Such companies became completely dependent on their computer systems for managing accounts and contracts. Engineers determine the company's strategy, organization, and development and plan the introduction of new products, even rebranding, because all "deliverables" in service industries are dependent on a chain of data processing.

THINKING WITH MODELS

In these circumstances, it is hardly surprising that the computer scientists' language and their way of representing the world have become the lingua franca of millions of white-collar workers around the world. This is especially true because simultaneously another dominant model was developed, project management, which called for a universal language to which everyone, from marketing to management, purchasing, technology, and sales, had to submit to understand and converse with a partner. Many company employees confirm the fact that organizations often had to adapt themselves to computer-derived modes of communication.

The hierarchically organized model of thinking presented, for example, in Microsoft's Windows Explorer, also found in PowerPoint, is well suited to employee communication in a company (see Conway's law, discussed in chapter 3). It is even more so for consultants, who are always preoccupied with quickly organizing their thoughts, summarizing them more tightly, and making them accessible to everyone. All consultants agree that this kind of formatting of thinking is a natural tool.

Hence, in some worlds, particularly in industrial, engineering, and computer sectors, the universal mode of communication has become the diagram, the matrix. It is not the tools of presentation that have created this situation. But software like PowerPoint no doubt facilitated and popularized the dominance of this type of representation.

In the view of some observers, the simplification and universalization characteristic of the use of these diagrams have had a catastrophic influence on thinking in companies. A former marketing director lived through the glorious age of presentations with glass slides, and she attacks this form of reductionism of thought:

> Diagrams kill thought! You can use them to illustrate an industrial process or a cycle, a circuit, but not a strategy! With PowerPoint, you're forced to formalize a thought by following a required and limited mold. Thinking has to adapt to a format; it's as though it were filtered, expurgated, leveled off. I don't think the models presented by consultants were always appropriate to the often serious issues to which they were supposed to recommend solutions. An organization is a living thing and in any case much more mobile and dynamic than images of fluctuations, cycles, arrows, flow charts, and the like.

Depending on managerial fashion and dominant styles of management, some kinds of graphs are used more or less frequently, evolve, or are abandoned as others are adopted for the long term. The same diagrams, more or less adapted to the circumstances, appear in the presentations of all consultants,

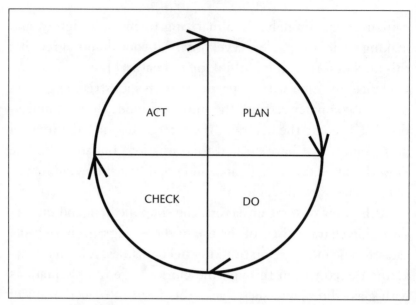

FIGURE 5 Example of Deming's wheel.

consumer survey firms, or sellers of ready-to-use slides on the Internet.[9]

Deming's wheel, for example, is a graphic representation of a method of quality-control management called PDCA (plan-do-check-act).[10] This diagram was devised by the statistician William Edwards Deming, who popularized it in the United States in the 1950s.

The four steps are planning, implementing, checking, and adjusting, following a single direction, each action bringing on the next, the whole intended to establish a "virtuous circle." PDCA makes it possible to improve the quality of a product or a service.

In the 1960s, other matrices began to flourish. In economics and management, a matrix is a model of economic analysis, usually represented by a table with n entries (often 2×2). Matrices are often named for their inventors, usually professors, such as

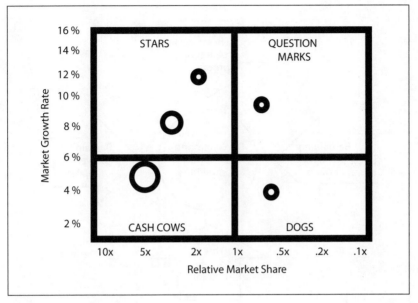

FIGURE 6 Example of BCG matrix.

Igor Ansoff, or consulting firms. Among the best known, the BCG matrix was created by the Boston Consulting Group.[11] It is intended to help managers decide what resources to allocate to one activity rather than another among a portfolio of activities, hence to define a company strategy.

Activities are distributed according to their market share and the potential growth of those markets into cash cows and dogs, stars and question marks. The company can thus decide which sectors are worth developing and investing in and which ones should be dropped. One can imagine how much this type of visualization—even backed by numbers—simplifies and brutally standardizes in an analysis leading up to a decision.

Other diagrams, through osmosis or because the term had a reassuring feel, adopted the name of matrix, even though they were different kinds of formalization, such as the "five forces" devised by Michael Porter. This Princeton-educated engineer got

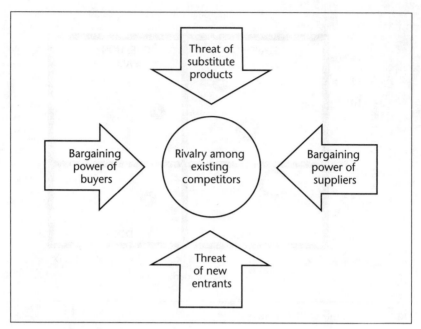

FIGURE 7   Porter matrix.

his doctorate in economics from Harvard in 1973. A star at the Harvard Business School,[12] he developed a theory of management intended to explain how a company obtains a competitive advantage by mastering more successfully than its competitors the forces structuring the market's environment. This mastery is illustrated by the implementation of a "value chain" that characterizes the company's economic model. In the 1990s, the notion of value chain became a key concept in the new management of organizations. Porter proposed a model in the form of five factors.

After identifying the key factors of success in relation to the economic environment, it is necessary to determine what are the first strategic actions to be taken to grow in the market. Many experts have discussed this model, which is still in use today. Some have criticized a rather military logic that consid-

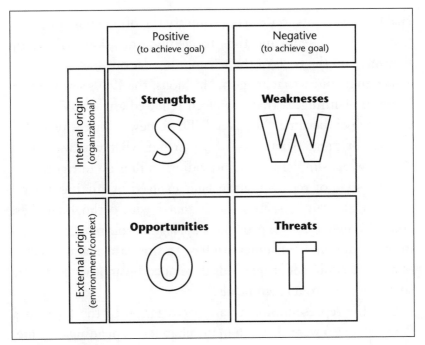

FIGURE 8 SWOT matrix.

ers threats, attacks, and defenses rather than collaboration, alliances, and opportunities.

Finally, there is another model, which has been served up in many varieties, the SWOT matrix, an acronym for strengths, weaknesses, opportunities, and threats, developed in the 1960s by four Harvard professors. It is intended to determine the strengths and weaknesses of a company and to consider the strategic choices to be made depending on different activities.

These models and matrices all come from different periods; they have been adapted for companies of various sizes, from various sectors, in diverse circumstances, and for variable goals; and they reflect heterogeneous philosophies of management. Nonetheless, they are the basic building blocks for many frameworks, made from mixing, stacking, and distorting them. They

enable consultants to formally simplify the often complex problems of their clients and thus to facilitate decision making by
managers on the basis of their recommendations.

When it comes to managerial fashions, the 1980s saw a "challenge to planning,"[13] that produced renewed attraction for matrices, which became "liberated." These new matrices provided
a sense of great flexibility—you can put what you want into
them—while simultaneously providing an illusion of rigor.

This style of representation later evolved by mixing several
types of diagrams—scatter plots, charts with orthogonal axes,
and 2 * 2 matrices—to produce *mapping*, a tool frequently used
in marketing and consumer studies. In this case again, a sector
of activity could adopt methods developed by another sector by
adapting them to its own needs.

Graphic representation of an organization in the form of a
flow chart also went through many changes, depending on time,
place, and habits. Along with the scientific organization of work,
the flow chart underpins rational and scientific organization.
The chart makes it possible to graphically promote certain types
of organization as being solid, stable, hierarchical, operational,
fluid, and so on. With the development of "human relations" in
the 1950s, the accent was put on interdepartmental relations. A
company was divided into different areas: processes, resources,
and relations. Representation of the company was affected, with
more atomized images and graphs in the form of trees, cubes,
and centered focuses, depending on the type of management
valued.

In the 1980s, a "project structure" (with a strong horizontal
bias) could be superimposed on the formal structure of the organization. The circle became an alternative to the usual tree
structure of the flow chart. Finally, in the 1990s, new agents—
experts—and new technological tools produced profound

changes in the way of drawing up a flow chart. Informal networks grew up, and the flow chart no longer described the reality of internal organization. Diagrams changed, using knots, chains, networks, and so on.

It is logical that these models should evolve over time, following changes in managerial paradigms. But over the years, these formalizations have constituted a visual grammar that represents and shapes organizational models for companies everywhere in the world. It is a universal language modeling the management of organizations, managers having adopted what must be called a dominant ideology. PowerPoint is the ideal tool to popularize and spread these models, particularly thanks to its own ready-to-use templates, and to catalog others for purchase on the Web or in banks of consultants' slides.

Curves, bar graphs, matrices, timelines, maps, pie charts, and Gantt charts all have become elements in an endlessly reproducible and combinable visual grammar. They also provide a scientific gloss for prepared messages whose real purposes are masked by a neutral-sounding discourse.

SLIDE "FACTORIES"

The consulting market was euphoric between 1994 and 2000. The coming of the year 2000, for example, was a bonanza for armies of consultants making sure that no breakdown would occur because of the computer bug that never materialized. During that period, the market grew increasingly international, and consultants became something like high-class temporary workers for some companies, where they managed strategic projects as outside contractors and were hired shortly afterward by their clients. These consultants were all paid per diem and evaluated on their contribution to the company's profits.

This encouraged them to bill the slightest service at ever higher rates.

The product sold by these consultants, advice, took the form of deliverables, primarily PowerPoint presentations, which became the basic value of these firms. The presentations enabled them to perform their expertise: propose plans of action, display their projects, and resell their "frameworks," their adapted ready-to-use organizational templates, modeled on presentations already used for other companies. For this purpose, they had teams able to master the tool and its grammar and banks of presentations, or they outsourced the production.

Consider two of the most famous companies in the sector, one a strategic consulting firm, the other an international investment bank, each an unquestioned leader in its field. Each in its own way, these two very discreet companies show how one can exercise considerable influence by conceiving and distributing models of thinking in the form of presentations.

Each meeting with a client, even the slightest work-related encounter between members of a project team, is a pretext for the design of presentations. First in the marketing phase, when the bank presents and proposes the potential transaction, there's the "strategic pitch." Then come practically daily exchanges with the client to update views on one point or another of the project. Finally, there are more formal presentations to decide on the implementation of the proposed transaction.

These documents are prepared from the outset in the form of presentations. All transactions, ranging from a simple letter of intent to the purchase or sale of a company, are settled by exchanges of slides, comparisons of tables of numbers, analyses of diagrams, comments on graphs, and so on. In general, discussion is based on very meticulously printed documents—there is no great difference between a working document and the final document for a formal presentation—and seldom on a projection, which makes the consultant less dependent on technical devices. This is particularly true in banking, which favors discussion with the client in his office, around a table with a few paper files, without constraints involving technical media devices. In these circumstances, contact is considered to be freer and more fluid; direct exchange is possible.

Each of the bank's projects is managed by a senior partner, flanked by two midseniors and a junior. It is usually the junior, assisted by one of the midseniors, who designs the slides, which he can send to be revised by a specialized group of graphic designers in a major European capital. This production group creates a very precise graphic chart that guarantees a minimum of homogeneity. It produces the bulk of final presentations for the sector, even though more and more consultants are able to create the most common presentations. The great majority of documents is in English. In some transactions, they can be translated into the local languages of the various countries where the bank does business.

The large American strategic consulting firm was founded between the world wars. Considered one of the most influential in the world, it advises the largest public and private companies in the world, as well as many governments. More than twenty heads of the largest international companies began their careers as consultants in the firm.

It is hardly surprising that the organizational models and strategic formulations conceived by this firm have penetrated through various channels, particularly through a powerful international network, into most large organizations. In addition, many of these consultants, who have become managing directors of companies they advised, have been able to spread the gospel of their ideas, models, methods, and tools to numerous institutions.[14]

This proliferation was made possible through the consultant's preferred weapon, PowerPoint. According to someone who has been a senior partner in the firm for fifteen years:

> PowerPoint is essential for the consultant as a communication tool. In many situations we have to transmit messages quickly in summary form. The PowerPoint format is very useful for presenting simple conclusions derived from complex analyses. To demonstrate something, it is simpler to draw a picture than to make a long speech. A diagram like a matrix enables the consultant to deal with any situation. It is very easy to squeeze reality into two dimensions, to give it meaning. An outline in two dimensions is more convenient for expressing or grasping an intuition.

In his view, one of the major assets of PowerPoint and the sequence of the presentation is its capacity to persuade on the basis of analogies:

> PowerPoint makes it possible to use the individual's analogical reasoning. You favor the setting up of bridges that would be completely forbidden or would seem ridiculous if they were expressed in a rational, verbal, or hypothetical-deductive mode. The use of analogy is a strength and a wonderful means of manipulation because it relies on a way of using the brain that no longer exists in a rational world, where you demonstrate, you reason by difference rather than by analogy.

These consultants also commonly use a technique of construction devised by Barbara Minto, a Harvard graduate and former consultant at McKinsey. This method of reasoning, known as the Minto pyramid principle, tree-shaped and inductive, enables consultants to construct an argument about any type of project. This simultaneously mechanical and visual technique, however, allows for no deviation or accommodation. It has to be followed strictly in order to be effective. Just as formal as the methods presented earlier, this method subtly puts together diagramming and language, making it possible to formalize ready-to-use speeches.

The firm has also established its "factory" for making slides. It has bent the software to its purposes by creating its own templates. Divided according to language groups, small teams in the company are specially assigned to make slides for consultants. These company studios sometimes call on freelancers for "express" productions.[15] Because of the industrialization of the process of fabrication and the homogenization of presentations around the world, the firm has also set up a center for the production of slides in India with fifty employees.

The firm has thus developed its own "customized" version of PowerPoint containing basic components as well as supplementary tools, graphs special to the firm, libraries of templates, preestablished diagrams, outlines created by the firm, and so on. The library is organized into two types of illustrations: graphs—generally numerical—and more "conceptual" drawings, timelines, and maps with captions made up of words and sentences.

With PowerPoint as the company's basic tool, all consultants are given training in the tools and formats specific to the firm. The structure, layout, and sequence of slides are identical: the title on top, a blue band and possibly photographs, a space for the client's logo. The rules of writing are dictated by a communications department, and all consultants are trained in the drafting of messages, the choice of the right graphs, and so on. An international company, the firm requires a single standard format with rules that apply everywhere. Each new version of PowerPoint is adapted and distributed to all branches.

Hence, throughout the world, every company, administration, and government advised by the firm dutifully contemplates the same succession of slides, developing their argument according to the same method, organizing the speech following the same thread, and telling the same stories. The ability to produce homogeneous and unique templates for the whole world no doubt represents a great strength of this type of firm. If the presentation is marked with a logo, standardized, and constructed according to a framework developed by decades of consulting for the world's largest companies, thereby profiting from a wealth of experience and best practice, success is automatic.

The legitimacy of this quantity of experience, the rationality of the demonstration, the graphic quality dripping with elegance and simplicity, and the talent exhibited by the staging and the speaker all encourage acceptance and establish the firm's reputation. The firm can win even the trickiest of competitions with a mere viewing of a presentation. This is all the more true because these firms often have a head start due to their formidable day-to-day knowledge of new management fashions and especially of effective methods of persuasion.

Among these effective procedures should be mentioned the technique of the executive summary, which again demonstrates the close complicity that exists between the technical medium, the way it is used, and the model of the argument. Along the lines of a movie or advertising pitch, the executive summary is for company management a summary intended to sell a project to financial and other interlocutors.

Anglo-Saxon consultants systematically tend to summarize

their conclusions in the first slides, a practice less common in Europe, where the preference is to present an articulated argument, a sequence in the speech, before leading to the proposition. In continental Europe, where the deductive style predominates, there is a tendency to lay out the presentation in the following manner:

- Why are we here?
- What is the problem?
- What is the context?
- What are the recommendations?
- The team
- The budget
- The timing and the deliverables

The audience then has to sit through the sixty pages of the presentation, hear about the quality of the reformulation of the brief by the consultants, the reasoning, the methodology, the CVs of the participants in the future mission, before coming to the proposition itself (or the conclusions in the case of a study).

Consultants in Anglo-Saxon firms use PowerPoint more for its summarizing aspects than as a rhetorical support. For them, it is more efficient to propose, in a limited time, a summary of results and recommendations for action than to solicit admiration for the unfolding of an argument. These consultants are trained to provide usable evidence of the relevance of their argument, not to exhibit the precision of their logic and methodology. The executive summary makes it possible to articulate a demonstration quickly, eliminating pages considered useless for the final outcome of the analysis. Hence, in a few slides, the client has an overview of what the consultants have observed and what they recommend.

So Anglo-Saxons prefer to start at the end and present their conclusions first. The senior partner quoted earlier, who has observed that this style of presentation is increasingly prevalent in the rest of the world, explains:

> It's no doubt unsettling, sudden, to begin with the conclusion. But we get to the point. Then we ask them to follow our reasoning to see whether it holds water. Brokers' notes work that way. A good executive summary helps managers make a complicated decision or one that is complex to approach by simplifying it to an extreme. How? By combining a certain number of ideas and then choreographing them. Or you can just focus on one or another point: if we're comparing market shares, the fact of putting it in the form of a slide, making a drawing, putting some ideas in parallel, is more forceful and more effective.

MAGIC TEMPLATES

Because the PowerPoint presentation is the only document delivered, certifying the concrete content of their service, these firms have communications "toolboxes" containing all the ingredients needed to fabricate it: images, complete sets of templates, storyboards, and so on. These tools are regularly updated and shared by experts in each branch around the world.

In 2003, PowerPoint supplied standard templates adapted to situations and goals: "managing organizational change," "selling an idea," or "creativity session." For example, six slides were suggested for "announcing bad news":

Current Situation
- Announce the bad news.
- Be clear, do not try to hide the situation.

How Did It Happen?
- History, appropriate facts or strategies.
- Original assumptions no longer valid.

Alternatives Considered
- Present the alternatives.
- Describe the pros and cons of each one.

Plan of Action Proposed or Final Decision
- Describe the plan of action proposed or the final decision.
- Explain how the plan of action proposed resolves the problem.
- Explain how the plan of action will make it possible to eliminate the problems caused by the situation.

Our Future Project
- Restate our goals.
- Define our future expectations.
- Establish a deadline for the expected results.

Summary
- Key points to retain that will give the audience confidence and boost its morale.

Aside from its summary character and the fact that its discourse is limited to pure paraphrase, this type of template represents in exaggerated form the way PowerPoint can transform a complex situation into a sequence of commands in a process. Thanks to the format, you confine yourself to a few vaguely programmatic messages, a few positive injunctions, or timidly mobilizing slogans in a serious situation. By following the model, you deliver none of the possibly expected messages. These templates intended to help construct a presentation operate more as banal prompters than as a real tool for argument. But according to communications experts, the simple fact of communicating *something* in a time of crisis is in itself a "strong sign" and makes it possible to "treat the problem" quickly, even if you have nothing to say.

These preformatted models also demonstrate that, thanks to a good PowerPoint presentation, one can deal with all kinds of problems. For example, another template suggests running a creativity session with these rules:

- All ideas are good.
- Be creative.
- Take risks.
- Avoid criticism.

This presentation, intended to enable each participant to exercise inventiveness and share it with partners, sets out a sequence of paradoxical injunctions: there is an authoritarian request to be creative, you are commanded to liberate yourself. This is one of the characteristic traits of the software's perversity, this ability to constrain everything while giving the illusion of freedom.

In the 2007 version, Microsoft abandoned its series of standard presentations and provided much more elegant functionalities: Smart Adds. This is a bank of ready-to-use graphs and diagrams where one finds, of course, all the elements needed to reproduce the usual models, such as matrices, radar charts, and scatter plots. There is therefore no need to rely on slides provided by consultants for an earlier study; you can concoct brilliant presentations on your own.

To replace the naive templates of the early days, Microsoft now makes it possible to download from a dedicated site "free models for office, home, and entertainment,"[16] multiplying categories and themes and applicable to all situations, the rule being that there are no contexts or circumstances to which PowerPoint cannot be applied.

The development of blogs and shareware has also fostered sharing and the free distribution of presentation templates to all comers. One of the best-known sites for sharing slides, a kind of YouTube of PowerPoint, is named Slideshare,[17] where unpublished presentations in every area are put online and shared every day. A final resource for "slide addicts": specialized sites market packs of thematic templates.[18]

The power of consultants is felt today in every area. The indispensable weapon for their mission is PowerPoint, which has greatly increased the influence of their models of thinking, to which the software has given form. Over time, because of technological advances and simplicity of use, these dominant models spread by PowerPoint have been propagated in business and beyond. They have thereby fostered a uniformity of discourse, standard ways of proposing, exchanging, and deciding that have continually invaded new territories.

7

UNIVERSAL CONTAMINATION

➡

PowerPoint quickly spread beyond the fields of economic activity and public relations. The growing influence of consultants in all sectors of activity and the dominance of a few software companies contributed largely to this omnipotence.

Historically, the military were the first major producers of tools for presentation and simulation, distant predecessors of Power-Point. But in a kind of boomerang effect, the army is now colonized by PowerPoint thinking, to the point that some American generals now think the software is their principal enemy.

PowerPoint has also contaminated the public sector, which has quickly fallen in step with the universal credo of profit making by using audits to import management models from business. Not to mention the field of human resources, where PowerPoint is one of the most frequently used modes of communication: not one negotiation, not one report of a union meeting, can be dreamed of without the use of a few slides.

SLIDE SHOW AT THE UN

On February 5, 2003, Secretary of State Colin Powell delivered one of the most famous PowerPoint presentations in the short history of the software. This presentation was intended to demonstrate the existence of weapons of mass destruction in Iraq and had to persuade public opinion and America's allies of the necessity for armed conflict against that country. In short, it was a preparation for war.

After a few opening remarks, Powell introduced his demonstration:

> The material I will present to you comes from a variety of sources. Some are U.S. sources. And some are those of other countries. Some of the sources are technical, such as intercepted telephone conversations and photos taken by satellites. Other sources are people who have risked their lives to let the world know what Saddam Hussein is really up to. I cannot tell you everything that we know. But what I can share with you, when combined with what all of us have learned over the years, is deeply troubling. . . . Indeed, the facts and Iraq's behavior show that Saddam Hussein and his regime are concealing their efforts to produce more weapons of mass destruction. Let me begin by playing a tape for you. What you're about to hear is a conversation that my government monitored. It takes place on November 26 of last year, on the day before United Nations teams resumed inspections in Iraq. The conversation involves two senior officers, a colonel and a brigadier general, from Iraq's elite military unit, the Republican Guard.

This theatrical introduction led into a PowerPoint presentation that relied on all the possible artifices provided by the software. The secretary of state piled up exhibits and various communication devices: audio recordings, video, satellite imagery, photographs, drawings, maps. In a dramatic flourish, he went so far as to exhibit vials allegedly containing Iraqi anthrax. Through powerful means of communication, Powell seemed to present real facts, even more palpable than photographs and maps.

One of the first attributes of PowerPoint, and not the least important, is its ability to produce multimedia presentations in a single medium: you can incorporate all types of audio and video files fluidly, with no effort, with a simple mouse click. You can also transport the audience from the Security Council to the middle of the Iraqi desert. But because the exercise in persuasion was not to be confined within the UN—indeed, Powell had to persuade the American people and all his allies—he used a second of PowerPoint's abilities: quick broadcast to the entire world. So after being posted on the White House Web site, the presentation appeared online a few hours after its delivery at the United Nations.

Flashback: on October 25, 1962, the American ambassador to the United Nations, the formidable orator Adlai Stevenson, forcefully questioned his Soviet counterpart about the existence of Soviet missile launchers in Cuba. In the face of Valerian Zorin's refusal to answer his question yes or no, Stevenson retorted, "I am prepared to wait for my answer until Hell freezes over. . . ." The former governor of Illinois and presidential candidate then staged one of the most memorable events to have occurred at the UN by having an easel set up at one end of the circular room where negotiations were being conducted. The famous pictures show an assistant standing in front of a flip-chart presenting large photographs to a large and attentive audience. Given the nature of the evidence—a series of aerial photographs reproducing the alleged locations of Soviet missiles on Cuban territory—it is doubtful whether spectators more than ten or twelve feet away could see anything clearly and judge the veracity of the evidence presented. However, these few blurry images seen at one end of a conference hall as large as a railway waiting room helped to avoid an escalation of the Cold War into a hot war.

Forty years later, Colin Powell's use of a PowerPoint presentation was not a matter of chance: "This deliberate parallel to Stevenson's address is one of the key underlying rhetorical strategies of Powell's demonstration."[1] A genuine threat revealed with panache can become an effective propaganda and indoctrination tool. Taking advantage of technological progress and multiplying digital theatrical effects by relying on the instantaneous display of the staged evidence—in short, going beyond Stevenson—Powell was almost certain of persuading the audience present, and he succeeded, with tragic consequences. The secretary of state, in an interview with ABC on September 8, 2005,[2] did not acknowledge that he had lied, and his performance will no doubt continue to be judged remarkable in the political history of the twenty-first century.

Colin Powell's performance has remained famous, but it represents only one episode, the most visible one, in the history of the often stormy relations between PowerPoint and the military in the United States.

If there is one area where images have acquired fundamental importance, that is in military intelligence. From antiquity, securing intelligence about the theater of operations, enemy positions on the ground, and the surrounding environment has occupied a central place: "With an image from distant observation and a predictive theoretical graph, we have, in the early seventeenth century, two precursors of the military use of imagery."[3] The army has indeed become a major source of inventions and patents that later spread to everyday life, as happened with the famous 3M transparencies discussed in chapter 1.

Having relied on aerial photography and radio transmissions in the early twentieth century, intelligence and especially military imagery experienced a remarkable leap forward with the emergence of computing. The first spy satellites were launched during the Cold War. In the United States, the National Reconnaissance Office (NRO) was established in 1960 to centralize all military and civilian (primarily CIA) needs for satellite reconnaissance. The National Security Agency (NSA) has its own satellites. In addition to infrared vision systems and panospheric and hyperspectral imaging, the military industry invented new ways of getting pictures, such as drones, remote-controlled flying robots able to collect information without risking the loss of human lives.[4]

With the development of the Internet and GPS, it is now possible to gain access to digitized battlefields onscreen, allowing soldiers to find in real time their location, their troop strength, the enemy's location, and their targets.[5] This means that basic military tactical maneuvers are pictured and even entirely scripted. As Patrick Quéau pointed out in 1985:

Electronic and computer images play a key role in the conduct of modern war. The military functions of the image are interesting to note, both from the perspective of the transformation of the practice of war and from that of their possible civilian applications. Seized by a feeling of urgency or threat, the military has been able to give new and essential roles to images. In doing so they have opened new pathways in the art of representation.

WAR ROOMS AND WAR GAMES

If it is now possible to make war by maneuvering troop movements on screens, it is also quite common for combat to be conducted virtually, in the framework of multiple sessions of *Kriegspiel* or war games conducted by the upper echelons of the American army to study different scenarios to be implemented in case of aggression or defense.

As the Iranian nuclear threat started to be mentioned during the 2004 American presidential campaign, *The Atlantic* decided to organize a war game simulating the preparation of an American attack against Iran.[6] The purpose was to study and reveal to the public the different options that would be available to a president of the United States in case of a conflict with Iran.

The origin of the *Kriegspiel* is owed to the Prussians—it spread to all European armies in the late nineteenth century—particularly to Baron von Georg Reisswitz, who presented it to the court in 1811. On a table representing the contours of the field of battle, wooden figurines symbolized military units. Rules governed the movements of combat units and effects of the terrain. The results of engagements were calculated with the help of resolution tables. In the late twentieth century, the same accessories were used when games of strategy became popular for a mass audience. The simulations were increasingly sophisticated and, with the advent of digital devices, spread beyond military activities. This was notably the case with politics: the 1994 documentary *The War Room*, for example, followed Bill Clinton's election campaign (see chapter 1). Some companies also use this type of simulation, known as a business war game, before responding to a request for proposals.

Military war games traditionally cover a wide spectrum of exercises, ranging from real maneuvers with actual troops on the ground to computerized simulations, including armchair exchanges between various actors playing roles. These exercises are intended to evaluate all aspects of a conflict, operational, strategic, diplomatic, emotional, and psychological, with the goal of providing optimal responses.

The exercise organized by *The Atlantic* took place in a meeting room and lasted three hours. The participants were all former high-ranking officers, intelligence experts, and high-level State Department officials, and all were fully entitled to propose options to the president, since they had earlier been in position to do that in reality. The experienced Sam Gardiner,[7] who ran the exercise, thought these games worked best if "the participants feel they are onstage, being observed": this makes them take their roles more seriously. The exercise was therefore videotaped.

To make the game as realistic as possible, Sam Gardiner obtained all the unclassified documents he could get his hands on. "His commitment to realism extended to presenting all his information in a series of PowerPoint slides, on which U.S. military planners are so dependent that it is hard to imagine how Dwight Eisenhower pulled off D-Day without them," James Fallows comments ironically. He goes on: "PowerPoint's imperfections as a deliberative tool are well known. Its formulaic outline structure can overemphasize some ideas or options and conceal others, and the amateurish graphic presentation of data often impedes understanding. But any simulation of a modern military exercise would be unconvincing without it."[8]

The game was a reconstruction of a working session as it might have occurred in the White House, the Pentagon, or any other strategic institution in the world. Not only was the meeting, with a presentation, role playing, and slides, staged as though it was a real working session, but the performance had a quasi-documentary purpose. Fallows has insisted on numerous occasions on the "reality effects" of the staging, the importance of the accessories that made it possible to attest to the realism of the experiment being conducted. It is as though he were staging the staging, along the lines of Al Gore's film. It is clear that this play within the play has a multiplier effect on the demonstration: the accessories seem indispensable to create a scenario that holds water and will trigger a decision. A declaration of war or an attack might well depend on good stage direction. The quality of the sequence and structure of the slides must give the impression of witnessing a news report, the dramatic structure of which has been carefully arranged. The only missing element is the voice-over.

Gardiner relied on a collection of eighty-four slides that used the same type of material as Colin Powell: maps, aerial photographs, satellite views, and so on, thus the same iconic and rhetorical tricks. The slides were sober, on a dark gray background, with spare texts: only the images were given prominence—rather bad-quality pictures, fuzzy, like paparazzi photos taken from a distance without the subject's knowledge. This procedure obviously accentuated the feeling of reality and authenticity. But each slide was open to interpretation: a group of buildings, one of which might be a nuclear reactor, another under which there might be a reservoir of heavy water, an area that looked like a uranium mine, a satellite photograph in which it was difficult to distinguish on a moonscape what might be warehouses, a truck carrying a rocket that "might contain chemical weapons," low-definition 3-D images illustrating the presence of mines in the Straits of Hormuz, and maps indicating the range of various possible weapons. In reality, every image represented what one wanted it to represent. The imprecision encouraged all kinds of interpretation, but being projected as documents accredited their legitimacy and hence their veracity.

At one point, the participants brought up a possible military intervention by Israel against Iran in the form of a preventive strike like the one Israeli Prime Minister Begin launched against the Iraqi Osirak reactor in 1981. This scenario had numerous flaws, particularly the fact that, unlike Osirak, a single target, the number of targets in Iran was unknown. Fallows comments:

> But for the purposes of our scenario, Israel kept up its threats to take unilateral action. It was time again for PowerPoint. Figure 2 shows the *known* targets that might be involved in some way in Iran's nuclear program. And figure 3 shows the route Israeli warplanes would have to take to get to them. Osirak, near Baghdad, was by comparison practically next door, and the Israeli planes made the round trip without refueling. To get to Iran, Israeli planes would have to fly over Saudi Arabia and Jordan, probably a casus belli in itself, given current political conditions; or over Turkey, also a problem; or over American-controlled Iraq, which would require (and signal) U.S. approval of the mission.

In conclusion, this war game devoted no fewer than fifteen slides to the plan of communication intended to accompany the operation. The same medium was used to deal with strategic questions (should we attack or not?), tactical issues (what flight plan should the planes adopt?), and the communication necessary to sweeten the pill for the American people: planning, principal messages in the form of bullet points, press campaigns and press releases, and so on. PowerPoint provides the extraordinary ability to mix three kinds of communication within a single medium: strategic, operational, and institutional. It accomplishes the feat of becoming, with a simple shift of focus, a powerful tool for decision making, action, and propaganda.

WAR.PPT: SLIDES AS THE ONLY WEAPONS

Essential for studying and setting up a military operation before-hand, PowerPoint has also become inescapable on the ground, particularly in Iraq.

In 2006, the journalist Greg Jaffe chose Camp Taji in Iraq as the scene of a report.[9] The article was intended to show the tensions between Iraqi and American troops. American advisers were trying to help the Iraqi army regain control over the country under the suspicious gaze of American troops stationed in the region. Iraqi officers and their advisers thought that the soldiers of the U.S. Army considered them "more like a problem than a partner."

Jaffe recounts months of tension that sometimes led to open disputes between the protagonists. These quarrels revealed serious problems of lack of communication and intolerance between Iraqi and American soldiers despite the advisers. Because of the constant presence of insurgents, the situation became extremely tense, to the point where Iraqi snipers targeted United States soldiers. Relations between the three principal protagonists—the supervisor of the American advisers, Colonel Charles Payne, a Colonel Saad of the Iraqi army, and Colonel James Pasquarette, who ran the camp—became poisoned.

In mid-March 2006, soldiers of Colonel Saad's regiment were killed by insurgent fire. Rather than allowing the Iraqi army to deal with the problem, Colonel Pasquarette's team called a meeting with colonels Payne and Saad and one of Saad's officers to present to them the plan he had concocted. According to Jaffe,

The two Iraqi officers were led through a 208-slide PowerPoint briefing, in which all the slides were written in English. The six areas the Iraqi troops were supposed to occupy were named for New England cities, such as Cranston, Bangor, and Concord. The Iraqi officers, who spoke only Arabic, were dumbfounded. "I could see from their body language that both of them were not following what was going on," says Maj. Bill Taylor, Col. Payne's deputy.

The two Iraqi officers had to wait for an interpreter to be able to express their disagreement and propose a different plan, which was rejected by the American colonel. A few months later, calm returned: the insurgents had simply moved away. But the squabbles continued until his superiors removed Colonel Payne, deciding that he did not have the skills needed for this work. In an interview, Pasquarette said he thought Payne had gotten too close to the Iraqi soldiers.

In *Fiasco*, his book on the invasion of Iraq, Thomas Ricks also indicts the modes of communication commonly used in the American army and the troubles they have caused. He describes, for example, a meeting between generals Tommy Franks and David McKiernan at the beginning of the Iraq offensive in 2003, a meeting intended to establish the plan of attack. The only document the two men exchanged was a slide Franks had received before the offensive from Secretary of Defense Donald Rumsfeld. This provoked an ironic commentary from McKiernan, reported by Ricks: "The way we do things nowadays is combatant commanders brief their products in PowerPoint up in Washington to OSD [the Office of the Secretary of Defense] and Secretary of Defense. . . . In lieu of an order or a frag [fragmentary] order, or a plan, you get a set of PowerPoint slides. . . . That is frustrating, because no one wants to plan against PowerPoint slides."[10] At the time, many people criticized Rumsfeld's fondness for facile and simplistic PowerPoint slides rather than clear and precise notes.[11]

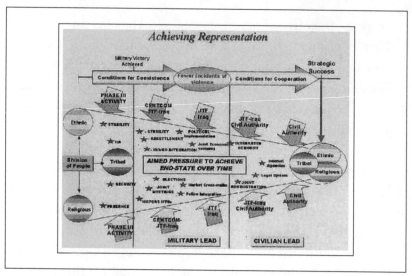

FIGURE 9 The plan for the occupation of Iraq.

In his book, Ricks dissects a slide titled Achieving Representation, which "explains" in a luminous diagram the organization of Iraq following the military operation.

From reading this slide, it appears that the internal affairs of Iraq are to be arranged in about forty months with five thousand American soldiers. The result seven years later was that almost a hundred thousand were still based in Iraq and the situation was far from stabilized.

All these anecdotes and edifying tales, often reported in newspapers, books, or specialized blogs, have led several high-ranking military officers to openly and vehemently criticize the common use of PowerPoint at all levels of the military hierarchy. General H. R. McMaster, who banned PowerPoint presentations when he led efforts to secure the Iraqi city Tal Afar in 2005, told Elisabeth Bumiller of the *New York Times*, "[PowerPoint is] dangerous because it can create the illusion of understanding and the illusion of control. Some problems in the world are not bullet-izable."[12] He was especially critical of bulleted lists, PowerPoint's real danger, because they take no account of the complex relations among political, economic, and ethnic forces. In the view of all these generals, the software program stifles discussion, critical thinking, and reasoned decision making. But they have watched anxiously and powerlessly as the bulk of the work of many officers has turned into the making of slides.

A platoon leader based in Iraq, Lieutenant Sam Nuxoll told a military Web site in 2009 that he spent most of his time "making PowerPoint slides. I have to make a storyboard complete with digital pictures, diagrams and text summaries on just about anything that happens. Conduct a key leader engagement? Make a storyboard. Award a microgrant? Make a storyboard."[13] And if these young officers don't know how to go about a presentation, they have specialized sites at their disposal, such as PowerPoint Rangers and Army Study Guide.[14] On the latter site there are presentations to download on "how to deal with prisoners of war," "how to lead an attack," and "how to use an M16." You can even learn how to behave during a nuclear attack, notably that you should "close your eyes." So the familiar expression "killed by PowerPoint"—commonly used to describe the sensation of numbness induced by a presentation—is not just hyperbole.

In an ironic way, superior officers attempt to hold their embarrassment in check by claiming that the software is especially useful when it is important to *not* communicate information, at press conferences, for example. But they can hardly deny the fact that PowerPoint has become the chief medium for every "killer brief" now indispensable for promoting one's ideas in the Pentagon.

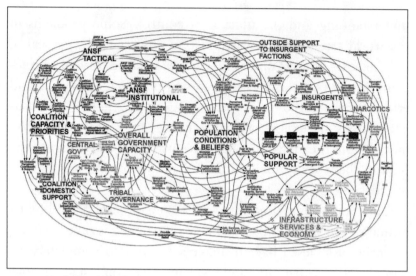

FIGURE 10　General Stanley McChrystal's "bowl of spaghetti."

At a U.S. Navy conference, a retired officer stated:

> Because briefing is the center of gravity, it has become vital for senior officers to develop subordinates who are skilled in this peculiar art of war. Because "the mission is the brief," the most valued attribute a staff officer can be blessed with is to be a "PowerPoint Ranger." The labels "innovative," "analytical," and "strategic thinker" are not used with the same sense of awe.

And he provided an example of a statement from one staff officer seriously claiming that "without my PowerPoint, I am useless," that in a war what counts is not information but the number of slides, the color of the highlights, and the format of the bullets, that "my PowerPoint and myself are defenders of my country."[15] This digital debauchery has in the last few years triggered much criticism within the military, where frantic computerization makes some fear a gradual loss of contact with realities on the ground.[16] Finally came General Stanley A. McChrystal's cry of alarm mentioned in the introduction of this book.

When he saw the slide meant to portray the complexity of American military strategy in Afghanistan, the commander of American and NATO forces remarked, "When we understand that slide, we'll have won the war." The famous PowerPoint slide that looks "like a bowl of spaghetti" became known around the world through a *New York Times* article published in April 2010.[17]

It is the army, major producer of and largest client for this type of presentation, that turns out to be its strongest critic. Like the executives of 3M who condemned the use of transparencies that they had propagated to the entire planet, the military has also realized that simplification and diagrams are perhaps not suitable for the serious problems it has to confront. As an American researcher has noted,

> These technologies such as PowerPoint perhaps point to a larger social phenomenon of the spectacle, and infusion of technology to reify our relationships to transactions. In this complicated, information dominated era, PowerPoint in some way mirrors a dumbing down and summary-like style of how lives are being lived, people being governed, and communications being executed. . . . It is critical that those within the government and bureaucracy understand the tools they are using when communicating and receiving information that applies to decisions of the highest importance.[18]

AUDIT IN THE MINISTRY; OR, HOW POWERPOINT PARTICIPATES IN THE REFORM OF THE STATE

RGPP: when he began his presidency, Nicolas Sarkozy engraved those letters on the title page of his political program. The *Révision Générale des Politiques Publiques* (General Review of Public Policy), officially launched in July 2007 in the aftermath of the presidential election, had goals on paper as ambitious as they were sensible: make the administration more effective for citizens while reducing public expenditure and valuing the work of public officials.

In reality, the RGPP reformulated for the public sector the dilemma of squaring the circle faced by so many private companies: how to improve the quality of service while reducing the resources to provide it. "The purpose, under cover of balancing the budget, was to make public sector services, such as hospitals, the postal service, research, and even education, profitable; it was also to provide niches of supplementary profitability to private companies," according to two union activists, authors of a book attacking what they call Wall Street management.[19] And indeed, at the same time it launched the RGPP, the government announced the pure and simple elimination of the posts of retiring civil servants.

The result: three years after its implementation, an opinion poll and a report submitted to the Budget Ministry demonstrated that more than 50 percent of the French population thought that their public services had gotten worse since the reform was implemented.[20] The major administrative reorganizations conducted at top speed, such as the creation of Pôle Emploi (combined employment service and unemployment benefit provider) in 2008, accumulated dysfunctions and critiques from users and experts.

But it is not so much the reform itself as the method by which it was sold and implemented, as well as the tools used, that I am concerned with.

Traditionally, organizational reforms of the state and of public services have followed a carefully managed process: inspectors general from all branches of the civil service are dispatched to the field to conduct investigations, to question agents, and so on. Reports are drafted to set out paths to improvement. The ones that seem least dangerous are then negotiated with union organizations. This very administrative process implicates agents, intermediate supervisors, and at the end of the chain, the top officials, as well as union organizations with which negotiations have been held to determine the measures, the personnel, and the costs involved. It is a long process simply because it involves negotiations, because if this slow mechanism is short-circuited, there is a strike, and the reform is not adopted.

The problem was how to secure acceptance of a policy of reduction when the parties involved knew that that would be possible only to the detriment of the quality of service. How could they secure the adherence of the participants, and especially how could they move as quickly as possible? The answer, according to a member of the cabinet staff: "By outsourcing the study and having it conducted by an auditing firm commissioned by the Ministry of Finance."

With the Finance Ministry in charge, the method, based on company audits, was supposed to produce rapid and visible results.[21] After an initial session in which a well-known firm proposed a vague methodology, outside consultants were sent into the field. Following a few face-to-face conversations with officials, these auditors quickly issued a diagnosis in a few slides, in which they generally suggested that departments with several hundred employees be reorganized. "For my service, for example, I never saw those auditors, although they were supposed to make high-impact recommendations.[22] I received their pack of PowerPoint slides by e-mail with no comments."

The document was indecipherable, and the logic of the

argument was extremely limiting. A former academic sociologist spent the night redoing the part that concerned her: "I was forced to stay within their framework, which meant I could not really develop my arguments. I had to formalize a target organization according to the table that the consultants had imposed on me by their formats. Nonetheless, I did add a slide of comments that were indispensable from my point of view."

In the age of the RGPP and the cult of budgetary rigor, this kind of proceeding has become widespread in public services. The method is a consequence of problems of internal resources: the rule of not replacing one out of every two retiring civil servants and the increase in supervisory positions—in government offices as in companies, there appear to be as many people to supervise as there are to perform duties—means that there are no resources left for such missions. According to an upper-level civil servant in a government department, "To economize, they prefer to use outside services instead of hiring a contract worker on a reorganization mission to help them over a period of two years to reorganize a department." Of course, using consultants is very expensive, but their mission lasts for only three months. As for private companies, the logic of externalization prevails primarily for cost reasons.

But the method has another advantage; harsh decisions are made by experts outside the department. It is a clever technique, already adopted in the private sector, that makes it possible to neutralize the risks of conflict at the source and to carry out a policy of quick and aggressive faits accomplis. Managers prefer to leave to others the acceptance of responsibility for reorganizations and reductions, the job of announcing bad news and then implementing it.

To manage to conduct an investigation in three months, establish a diagnosis, and draft a recommendation, in a sector and about jobs that they are unfamiliar with, these consultants have to apply methods already used elsewhere. And they already have everything in house; they just have to adjust the investigation and adapt the deliverable. "The value of PowerPoint is that in two clicks, where there was Budget of Department X, the next day you can write 'Regional Office of Y': you 'customize,' 'localize' your presentation," according to the civil servant quoted above.

Hence, out of concern for efficiency and speed, audits developed and written for specific needs in other sectors—notably the private sector—are adapted, presented, and sold to officials who have developed the habit of buying standard services that are often very formalized. This system is reassuring for the auditing firm, which already has everything in its project documents and for the decision maker, because everything is carefully framed, calculated, and planned out. The way the market operates, from the initial brief to the request for proposals, is completely standardized: the proposal is worked out together—for example, the number of interviews, the working groups, the number of managing committees, the frequency of staff meetings per week, and so on. The client has nothing to do but check boxes in the PowerPoint presentation.

This standardization is one of the key elements of the RGPP, which wants to impose the same standards everywhere, upstream as well as down, that is, both in initial methodology and in grounds for decision and deliverables. It is the best way of demonstrating to the Ministry of the Budget that a particular system of reference will be put in place, that certain indicators will be implemented, that one or another measure will be acted on. Visually accredited, the result becomes tangible. The content of the reform, its organizational intelligence, and its human impact are of little importance. The only things that count are the description (the pitch), the budget, and the deadline, each in a few bullet-point lists.

But PowerPoint falls far short of the standards of rigor of documents prepared by the public administration. In those institutions, every item has to be traced, referenced, sourced. The subjects studied are barely skimmed by the service providers present for a few days. To work quickly, they are forced to select scraps of information, bits of documents, and fragments of data. All that counts is piling up facts. On their slides adorned with their logos, there are no sources, no authors, and no references for excerpts. These PowerPoint presentations have neither status nor audience nor author. The civil servant says, "That's why they can be used for everything and nothing."

That is the ambiguity of this type of document, simultaneously a report, a summary note, an aid to communication, an aid to decision making, and a rhetorical assistant. A single document for everything: productivity is maximized with the advantage of a flexibility that makes it possible to adapt the medium to various contents. It legitimates sometimes questionable decisions, while relying on procedures that are, to say the least, simplistic.

This confusion of status preserves the authoritative character of the content of a presentation. Because of its anonymity, a PowerPoint deliverable offers no possibility of exchanges or debate, whereas a note can be a tool for helping to make a decision that one can criticize or challenge. Through its patchwork appearance and its anonymity, a PowerPoint presentation avoids raising the questions that are the basis of thinking: Whom does it address? Who signs? What are the sources? What is the goal? For what type of written document? In a PowerPoint presentation there is nothing to demonstrate, to think about; you just have to follow the lists.

Foreign researchers have been troubled by the dangerous liaisons in methods between private consultants and government services. Is it justifiable for states to use the methods and models of management of the private sector, which is far from having the same goals? As the Canadian researcher Denis Saint-Martin observes,

> In the course of the last twenty years, management consultants have become increasingly visible participants in the process of reform of the public sector. . . . In Australia, one study went so far as to say that consultants had "reoriented" the sociopolitical framework of the country, while in France a former industry minister (Roger Fauroux) has claimed that a cabinet minister arriving at a meeting with a report from McKinsey or the Boston Consulting group resembles "Moses coming down from the mountain with the Tablets of the Law."[23]

This grip of consulting in the public realm has a clearly North American origin: "Consultants have always participated more actively in the development of policy in Washington than in any other capital in the developed world." This fact helps "explain a large number of the discussions about the 'Americanization' of management practices in the private and public sectors."[24] France, it seems, had been able to resist this Americanization, thanks in particular to the presence of high-ranking civil servants trained in the *grandes écoles* for French engineers at Sciences Po and the École Nationale d'Administration. But under the ideological hammer blows of Anglo-Saxon neoliberalism in the 1980s, private intervention in the public sphere has increased. "Starting in the 1980s a change occurred: under the influence of the ideas of 'new public management' and the rise of the 'new right,' governments in search of the greatest effectiveness began to depend on outside consultants for the transfer of ideas and management practices from the business world to the public sector."[25]

North American in origin, the model has become global and the standards identical. For auditing accounts, for example, whether the auditors are from Deloitte, KPMG, or Ernst & Young, the same methods are used in the United States, France, and Germany. Adaptations are made to the legal context, but in the background, the same recipes are used, perfectly suitable for multinational companies. The same methodology applied to all subsidiaries in the world enables all types of comparisons and especially the award of excellent marks from the world's financial rating agencies. A cabinet official comments ironically: "Why hire international firms and not the small local firm of experts? Because the international firm is a little like McDonald's. Whether you're in New York, Paris, or Tokyo, it's the same Big Mac. It's probably not the best hamburger in the world, but you're sure to be eating something that has the usual standard taste."

Public services in general have been drawn into this process of standardization intended to make them constantly more effective, more efficient, and less costly. The problem is that public hospitals or the postal service are not multinational companies with subsidiaries that can be evaluated, compared, and rated month after month. Of course, some indicators spread out on a stack of PowerPoint slides can marginally help improve some processes or save some expenses, but they can by no means guarantee the quality of the service rendered or employee acceptance of reforms. The cabinet official says:

Sixty to eighty percent of our daily activity cannot be evaluated through deliverables or by measurements of volume and therefore cannot be shown in slides. Of course, you could say that accounting can display the number of bills employees have paid. Why not? That would provide the volume of transactions, but would you see all the budgeting work that went on beforehand, for example? There are entire fields of activity that would never be made visible.

MANAGING "HUMAN RESOURCES"

Like all areas of company administration, the human resources department, which used to be known as personnel management, has also come under the influence of PowerPoint.

The presentation software has become ubiquitous in negotiations and presentations of company "restructuring" or "job-saving" plans (*plans de sauvegarde de l'emploi*, or PSE),[26] in other words, to all social plans, in managerial Newspeak. A young HR consultant comments: "In selling a PSE, PowerPoint is ideal for distributing the key messages and especially for evading the issue." Indeed, human resource directors (HRDs) systematically rely on the software to sell any restructuring to the various stakeholders in the company.

In France, a PSE has to be communicated to the employees' council (*Comité d'entreprise*, or CE) in a twofold procedure of information and consultation. The first procedure—legally known as Book IV—concerns the various elements of the restructuring plan and its economic aspects. The CE receives all the information that will enable it to formulate an opinion. The second procedure involves consultation by the CE of Book III, which justifies the layoffs and specifies the measures accompanying the plan. Whereas the consultation of Book IV is little regulated, that of Book III is subject to strict verification deadlines. In addition, the CE can ask for the assistance of an outside expert—generally a firm associated with the majority union in the company—paid by the employer, to obtain more thorough analyses of the plan.

These "books" are usually fairly dense documents in Word format. But they are also presented in PowerPoint summaries during various negotiation sessions. For instance, a carefully drafted, rather technical legal document can be presented in the form of bullet-point lists, tables of figures, arrows, calendars, and diagrams. Through the magic of a few cleverly designed slides, some decisions can be buried under serious material showing rigorous work, especially that all the economic alternatives have been explored. Indeed, it is customary that a social plan be treated like any other company project, with the same tools and the same language. Models and methods have to conform to corporate language.

To stick closely to the standard models of company presentation, further guaranteeing its legitimacy, the presentation usually begins with the economic context and the social situation, followed by the legal framework, relations between the company and union representatives, and accompanying measures. As often happens in French-style presentations, sensitive information is placed at the end of the document, just as in a commercial presentation the budget and the resources used are found at the end. The entire manipulation consists of selling an extraordinary event in the ordinary format as though it were in the usual course of business of the company.

Expert reports consulted by the CE also adopt this framework and use PowerPoint. Indeed, for some years now, the ideological suspicion unions have of company experts has led them to call on specialized firms. One of the earliest of them, Syndex, was created in 1971 by young certified public accountants and statisticians to enable employee representatives to gain a better economic understanding of their company. In the 1980s, the profile of these experts changed considerably, from militant accountants to "neutral" experts with specialized degrees.

> Many of them had held human resources positions, or jobs in business, traditional consulting, or marketing. New hires at Syndex did not join the firm, as the founders had, "to serve the people." They wanted to have a professional career. They did not identify themselves as "militants" but as "interveners." . . . These experts from another generation required a high degree of professional rigor, as indicated by their effort to standardize the methods of intervention. . . . Unlike the experts of the 1970s, who identified with the figure of the organic intellectual, the model for the new entrants was the professional adviser who, like management advisers, operated as a service provider.[27]

It should be said that the 33,000 CEs have become a huge market for these consulting firms, which now provide extended services to elected employee representatives. Employee representatives also want to have a better grasp of the decisions of employers and thus understand the economic environment. In short, they want to be able to fight on an equal footing with management, especially because management does not always make their job easy. "First of all, the work of the elected representative takes place in circumstances marked by urgency. The strategy of employers often favors holding information back and making announcements at the last minute. In restructuring plans, for example, employee delegates need information and diagnoses that they can use quickly."[28]

HRDs have also found specialized firms to assist them in these proceedings, particularly in restructuring plans. Firms like Altedia, Eurogroup, BPI, Algoé, and Cegos have seen increased business in the last ten years. Unlike accounting firms like Syndex, these generalists in human resources (training, recruitment, and so on) intervene to implement the process of counseling employees who will be forced to change position, status, job, or work site or to leave the company and be transferred elsewhere. These are complex operations that often require the intervention of government authorities. These firms can participate at various levels, and they are often dependent on the HRD and his maturity on the question, considering that one of the skills most sought after for those holding that position is previous experience in conducting a PSE.

HRDs call on the firms to implement a PSE and the follow-up of displaced employees, usually in the form of a request for proposals. According to a former human resources consultant: "In a request for proposals, there are often many firms, and our first proposal has to be 'sexy.' There are training programs to make this kind of presentation." Proposals are often articulated in the same way, with more or fewer headings depending on the firm and the client. Here is an example:

- The context
- The client's problem
- Our understanding
- Our methodologies
- Our philosophy
- Our principles of action
- Detailed description of the proposal
- Staff and organization of the project
- Budget

Is it a combined effect of the tool and of the techniques of neo-management? In any event, a PSE is sold like an ordinary consultation or the launching of a product. To be sure, in the way it is presented, a social plan is akin to setting up an organization, a service, or new procedures, like any company project. But the rigorous presentation of a PSE slips toward sales talk, accentuating the "strong points," the "key concepts," the "criteria" to be remembered, using a whole panoply of points and bullets. Information provided to employee delegates is imperceptibly transformed into a sales pitch. It is hardly surprising that this demonstration is taken in hand by professionals in "social" communication.

What message is sent to the personnel? What will they make of it? For one HR consultant, the quality of the discourse is clear: "Management doesn't want to hear about people. It wants to hear only about procedures. The personnel do not exist and the company says that very clearly in the form of slides. PowerPoint says it so the managers don't have to." We can agree that it is hard for anyone who "brings about change" to have his legitimacy accepted by the ones who are subject to that change. Thanks to devices with precise numbers, arcane diagrams, and triumphalist slogans, PowerPoint enables decision makers to make what is happening less alarming and to distract personnel from its real nature. According to the consultant, "It's really a kind of magical thinking: PowerPoint objectively governs the relation between the person who holds power and the one who does not. The presentation clearly states that there are not and there will not be any interactions. On the contrary, it creates distance. PowerPoint enables its users to avoid paying attention to the people sitting in front of them."

With PowerPoint, no one is really speaking, but an entity emits orders and declarations. The software takes the place of the speaker by mutual consent. Through this distancing effect,

PowerPoint creates a screen—like the screen memories explored by psychoanalysts—that removes responsibility from decision makers and openly declares that their margin of autonomy is limited. In other words, the only way to exist in these conditions is to say: as an organizer of the social plan, I have no room to maneuver that would allow me to do more than manage the plan like any other industrial project. It's only a matter of applying good management methods, i.e., limiting costs and reducing negative consequences for the organization, and especially for the individuals concerned.

PowerPoint fosters and clearly expresses this strategy of evading the complexity of problems by always reducing arguments to the utmost simplification. "PowerPoint involves a bit of confusion between political discourse and political project. PowerPoint has the function of political discourse that takes the place of a project: since you have said it, that takes the place of a program, whereas implementing the discourse involves unbelievable complexity," according to the expert quoted above, a fierce opponent of this conditioning. And conditioning is the appropriate term, especially when the device becomes a process that spreads to the remotest corners of the management of human resources.

"ACTIVATING" ACCORDING TO FRANCE TELECOM

Beyond the PSE, PowerPoint has become practically the only vector for communication involving social relations with the company personnel: transfers, training, recruitment, evaluations, and so on.

France Telecom, long a model in the management of human resources, has seen its social reputation seriously eroded in the last few years. In September 2009, a wave of suicides[29] among the telephone company's employees was beginning to trouble the authorities so much that Minister of Labor Xavier Darcos summoned the head of the company, Didier Lombard, to his office. The Web site Bakchich managed to get a copy of a presentation of fifty-six slides intended for France Telecom managers.[30] This PowerPoint presentation is a model of the methods and gimmicks of fashionable neo-management, particularly at France Telecom.

This training program was designed by a consulting firm, Orga Consultants, subsidiary of an important French IT services company, Sopra Consulting, experts in management and technological consulting. The firm defines its primary mission in these terms: "We assist our clients in their major programs of change. The solutions we propose are as diverse and concrete as the problems they are devoted to solving: establishment of new services, optimization of processes, industrial organization, development of sales performance, elaboration of IT strategies, design and implementation of information systems, motivation of personnel."[31] Optimization of processes, sales performance, and motivation of personnel—quite a discordant mixture.

The document is from 2007, at a particular moment in the history of the French institution of telecommunications. France Telecom had for a few years been undergoing a considerable change in its economic model, due particularly to the technological explosion (in telephony and the Web) and increased competition in a market where it once held a monopoly. This transformation affected the strategic decisions of the company and the constant reorganizations carried out by successive CEOs, Michel Bon followed by Thierry Breton.

The privatization of the public utility began in the late 1980s. The monopoly came to an end in 1996. As head of the company from 1995 to 2002, Michel Bon was confident that he could turn the venerable business into a modern company, flexible, profitable, efficient, and innovative. His policy was simple: to counter the competition, landline prices had to come down and services improve, mobile and Internet services had to be developed, and the company had to become multinational. All this came at the cost of monstrous indebtedness (€68 billion in 2002) approved by a state that had less and less say in the matter. This triumphalist policy led to the loss of thousands of employees (almost forty thousand jobs abolished between 1999 and 2003), early retirements, forced transfers (seven hundred annually at one point), and changes in status—from civil servants to private employees. Successive managers tried everything to improve productivity, increase profits, remain in the forefront, and especially transform company culture, accused of being attached to its privileges and immobile. The key word in France Telecom became *mobility*.[32]

The presentation by Orga Consultants was part of a vast training program offered by the France Telecom management school. Imposed on the four thousand managers identified in the company in a program to promote its key employees, the program was made up of six modules spread over ten days of training in a period of nine months. The issues at stake in the training as a whole were summarized in a preliminary series of slides showing the company's economic circumstances: decline of the landline market, change in the business model turning partners into competitors, low productivity, and finally a disastrous age pyramid. The picture was bleak.

The exemplary sequence of the demonstration is shown in six sequential slides on pages 183–185.

This sequence of slides builds a scenario and a form of dramaturgy: market slowdown and cacophony among players followed by a decline in productivity and an "unbalanced" age pyramid.[33] This very fluid progression, encouraged by PowerPoint, makes

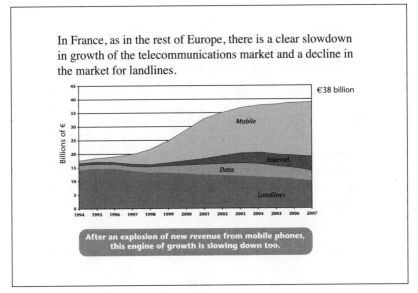

FIGURE 11 The telecommunications market.

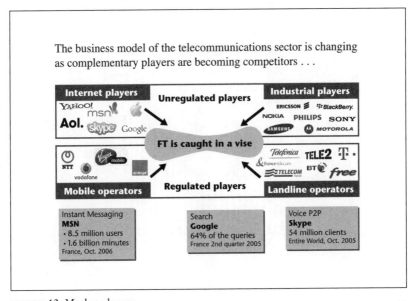

FIGURE 12 Market players.

Our productivity, growing constantly, remains one of the worst among European operators

	Revenues / Employees by country (K€)	
	2004	2005
France Telecom	221	240
Deutsche Telekom	203	244
British Telecom	275	273
Telefonica	310	326
Telecom Italia	326	330
Vodafone	666	703

FIGURE 13 Comparative productivity of various players.

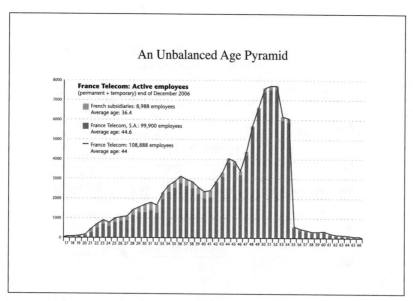

FIGURE 14 Age pyramid.

To confront these business challenges, FT has decided to deploy **ACT**: the HR section of NExT (New Experience in Telecom Services) to:

• improve our productivity

• adapt our existing skills to new jobs

• provide the maximum possibility for external hiring

• make our age pyramid younger

• provide new opportunities for professional development to our employees

FIGURE 15 The HR plan.

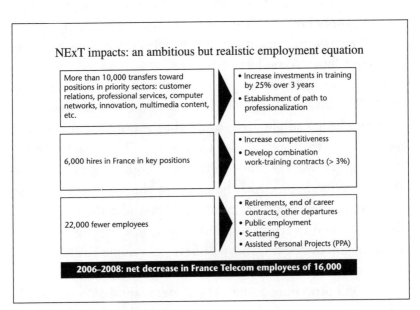

NExT impacts: an ambitious but realistic employment equation

More than 10,000 transfers toward positions in priority sectors: customer relations, professional services, computer networks, innovation, multimedia content, etc.	• Increase investments in training by 25% over 3 years • Establishment of path to professionalization
6,000 hires in France in key positions	• Increase competitiveness • Develop combination work-training contracts (> 3%)
22,000 fewer employees	• Retirements, end of career contracts, other departures • Public employment • Scattering • Assisted Personal Projects (PPA)

2006–2008: net decrease in France Telecom employees of 16,000

FIGURE 16 Impacts of the HR plan.

it possible merely through the sequence of slides to avoid a more thorough demonstration and thereby to arrive at the plan proposed in the HR section in figure 15, and then more pragmatically in the slide in figure 16.

The goals of the plan envision a "net decrease of 16,000 employees between 2006 and 2008." The Human Resources Department, however, does not hesitate to observe later on that this policy, which involves getting 10,000 employees to move, hiring 6,000, and getting 22,000 to leave, imposes a "dynamic of abrupt change." That's the least that can be said, even if France Telecom seems to have been accustomed for more than a decade to badly organized management. The presentation casts the logic governing the preparation of the plan in a brutal light. The sequence forces acceptance of the chain of arguments that brook no contradiction thanks to their staging.

The module published by Bakchich relies basically on practical examples, divided into three parts: "what strategy for activating?" meaning how to tell an employee that he has to "move" or leave, "how to implement it"; "work out one's managerial posture"; and "how to conduct exchanges."

A series of slides is designed to react to "postures of resistance." For instance, one colorful slide illustrates the bad reactions employees might have when they are told that they are going to have to change workplace and job. This is the first stage of a sequence with bubbles and comic strips designed to look like direct quotations, real thoughts "in the field," and thereby to show the company's desire to really consider the employees' discomfort and to try to respond to it. It is a "strong" message intended for managers who will have to assume responsibility for the decisions of their superiors.

A second procedure fostered by PowerPoint makes it possible to put the program into diagrammatic form. Even in rudimentary

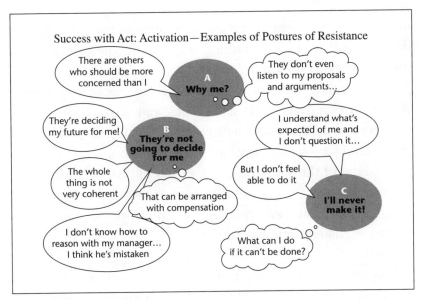

FIGURE 17 "Bubbles" of resistance.

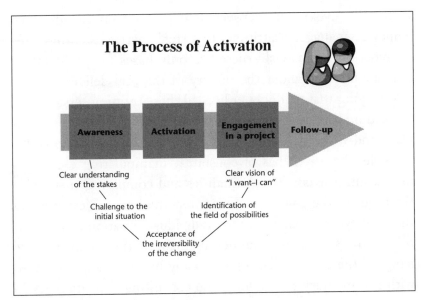

FIGURE 18 Formalization to reassure.

form, these formalizations make it possible to make the procedure rational, to turn it into a quasi-scientific proposition in a
highly emotionally charged situation.

The training program closely resembles a sales action plan,
with its arrows, stages, goals, messages, and slogans (Awareness,
Activation, Engagement in a project") and its vague sequences of
managerial jargon (anticipation, strategic vision, sense of initiative). Many of the slides function as lists of process commands.
PowerPoint can thus operate as a means of reducing tension
designed to change an emotional situation into a "process," a
human exchange into a managerial method, an instrument of
catharsis.

PowerPoint successfully plays its role as a management tool
that constantly tries to blur the boundary between the social and
the psychological in order to control individuals. Depending on
the need, the human resources consultant becomes a personal
coach or even a therapist, proposing behavior modifications
with titles evoking pop psychology—"work on the distance
employee-manager," "attitudes to foster," "active listening," "reformulation." Obviously these are only bases for presentation
that say nothing about the quality of the oral delivery or the
role-playing that no doubt enlivened these training sessions.

Reading this advice, this managerial discourse that runs on in
black-and-white slide after slide, gives one chills. There is, for
example, the way it has of constantly manipulating exchanges
by praising the employee's qualities and comparing them with
the needs of the company. This often amounts to destabilizing
the employee by balancing his individual situation against his
role in the system and the development of the company. The
icing on the cake is that, carried away by its Newspeak mixed
with rudimentary psychology, the consulting firm indulges in

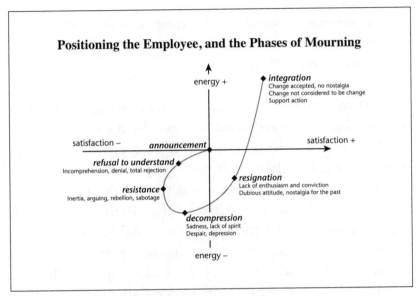

FIGURE 19 A rope to hang yourself with!

discursive and graphic shortcuts with a slide titled "Positioning the Employee, and the Phases of Mourning."

As the Bakchich reporter writes, "at a time when France Telecom was already aware of the question of suicides linked to constant restructuring (the company was in the midst of the Next plan aimed at abolishing 22,000 jobs between 2005 and 2008), one can appreciate this graph in the form of a hangman's noose. It seems even consultants have an unconscious."[34] Beyond the tragic irony (and the graphic Freudian slip), and beyond the particular situation of France Telecom, it is as though PowerPoint made it possible, through the power of its graphic rhetoric, to put in place means of glossing over the shocks that the social measures proposed cannot fail to provoke. Here too, the software offers itself as a tool for evasion and distancing. The presentation meets the needs of managing directors, who seem to assume responsibility for their decisions, but without committing themselves, and of managers forced to deal with situations they did not create.

Army, state, personnel management: three related areas that have been gradually "PowerPointed," seldom for the better, usually for the worse. The software is useful for presenting measures that harm people as though they were simple organizational processes responding to economic necessities and therefore rational and legitimate. Unlike its use in sales and spectacle, PowerPoint removes emotion and establishes distance. By the same token, it makes it possible to continue disseminating *la pensée unique* (neoliberal orthodoxy) with its values of simplicity, speed, efficiency, and so forth—while masking the responsibility of its perpetrators and continuing to charm victims mesmerized by the beauty of numbers and curves.

8

AT SCHOOL WITH POWERPOINT?

➡

Faced with the turbulence of the 1970s and 1980s, companies radically changed their organization and adopted new forms of management. If a company wanted to be more efficient and competitive, it had to wager on "human capital." According to the definition of the Organisation for Economic Co-operation and Development (OECD), *human capital* means the "stock of knowledge, qualifications, skills, and individual characteristics that facilitate the creation of personal, social, and economic well-being." Initiated by the American economist Theodore Schultz, the expression was popularized by Gary Becker, a student of the monetarist economist Milton Friedman[1] who applied a rational economic model to explain various aspects of human behavior. Becker won the Nobel Prize in Economics in 1992 "for having extended the domain of microeconomic analysis to a wide range of human behavior and interaction, including non-market behavior."[2]

Composed of skills, experience, and knowledge, human capital is acquired through education, preserved by use, and developed through training. It is assumed to produce benefits for both the individual and the company, which profits from increased expertise. To meet this need, organizations began to develop training policies. In the 1970s, continuing professional training became a permanent feature of French companies. Trainers at first used the tools of traditional teaching (though replacing blackboards with flip-charts), but in the 1990s, PowerPoint gradually took over as the favored medium for professional training.

University professors quickly understood the value of Power-Point for initial training. Slides that could be sent by e-mail replaced old-fashioned transparencies within a few years. Power-Point took over American and then European campuses around the mid-1990s. Then, driven by public policy, the new technologies, in different forms and with varying degrees of intensity, entered secondary schools.

Without stigmatizing in principle the use of new technologies, one might wonder at what point the school environment will resemble that of a company in the service sector, with every child sitting at a workstation, eyes riveted to a screen. It is impossible not to fear that future schoolchildren will be conditioned by a panoply of technological tools that, in the long run, might well deeply alter time-tested pedagogical methods. Wouldn't this be a way of following the logic of "lifelong learning"[3] and the surreptitious intent of imposing by school age the tools of neoliberal management? In any event, it is hard not to dread this nascent "PowerPointing" of minds in places dedicated to learning and the transmission of knowledge.

TRAINING IN COMPANY LOGIC

Instituted by law in 1971 and dispensed by a variety of organizations, continuing professional training is financed in France jointly by employers, the state, and local communities. Overall expenditures in 2009 for continuing education and training amounted to more than €27 billion (1.5 percent of GDP), more than 40 percent covered by companies, and almost 50 percent by the state and localities.[4] Of the €16.5 billion in direct training expenses (teacher pay, engineering, counseling, and so on), training companies take in about €10 billion.[5] In constant progression for some years, the market is relatively concentrated. The largest firms—often the heavyweights of Human Resources, such as Cegos and Altedia—account for almost half the revenues. Following the same developments as for companies, particularly in technology, training methods have deeply changed in the last few years, often in questionable ways.

Depending on the type of training, practitioners use—or not—media. According to Florence R., a former trainer in the company: "In Cegos we didn't use them much. That was tied to our 'personal development' method and a little atypical. We had media for times when we presented key concepts. But basically we worked with practical exercises, case studies. Media were used for reconstructions and debriefing."

Training organizations gradually had to adapt to the demands of their clients. They started to prepare modules made up exclusively of long series of boring slides to meet the needs of companies that swore by nothing but PowerPoint. Large firms formatted their methodologies, lavishing the same management recipes on company after company. According to Marie-Anne L., a training consultant, "Those firms sold a managerial 'toolbox' where the whole mechanism was intended to smooth out language, standardize it, simplify and normalize situations. All the preparatory work of thinking was reduced and concentrated onto PowerPoint."

This dynamic changed the professional structures of training, particularly in that training programs were increasingly dispensed by people outside the profession. Whereas the original presentations by firms were generally designed by training engineers, they were subsequently produced in large numbers by temporary employees who were not trainers by profession. The use of PowerPoint turned out to be very economical: modules took much less time to prepare and teach.[6] A completely adaptable digital medium, PowerPoint files can be copied, recycled, divided into parts. In addition, trainees have a document that testifies to their participation in the training program, something they can take back to their offices—although it often ends up at the bottom of a drawer.

Training programs have followed a path of development linked to the sociology of companies, in step with managerial and ideological fashions. In the 1970s, companies became aware that employees were not simply "hands" but that they also had brains and feelings, so training programs emphasized individual "creativity" and personal expression. In the 1990s, the fashion was for "process" and "reporting," reflecting an increasingly financialized view of the company. Training programs joined the post-Fordist bandwagon: modules talked about "time management," "project management," "performance indicators," "leadership development," and so on.

The effect of this discourse of creativity centered on the autonomy of the employee, along with the systematic use of PowerPoint, was that company managers often tended to shirk their role as educators and guides. As long as an employee presented a document certifying that she had attended a presentation, managers determined that they had done their work of providing information and training. One trainer comments, "It's a way of sloughing off, creating the illusion that people know what they have to do." PowerPoint also brings out the atomization of organizations. "During training sessions, each individual concentrates on his part and avoids his responsibility for the project as a whole. An overall view of the purpose of what is presented is never seen. Each individual works on segments of the whole and has only a fragmentary view of projects." PowerPoint makes it possible to split up activities into a series of tasks. Florence comments, "In a project, you think there are horizontal connections, but each individual is selected for his expertise and stays within his area of activity. The project mode thus becomes a new form of Taylorism."

This intensive use of PowerPoint in training programs has also had effects on pedagogical practice that have sometimes been harshly criticized by professional trainers. A training and placement consultant after having been a marketing manager, Marie-Anne L. was never really taken with PowerPoint: "My way of working is above all centered on the emergence of meaning from the thinking of people brought together in a group." She now works a good deal with the public sector and provides coaching advice. Her approach is very different from that of the large firms: "I refrain from all expected guidelines, any theoretical reference, any preestablished model. In a training session, I use very few media devices."

She is, however, forced to make presentations to "reassure her clients," including those in the public sector, where training curricula contain large file folders full of PowerPoint presentations. But like most trainers I have met, Marie-Anne favors shared writing on flip charts: "Writing down ideas expressed by the group allows for more exchanges, mobility, dynamism. That avoids the hypnotic and soporific effect of slide projection that is the number-one enemy of the trainer. When you come back to a fourteen-hour presentation to a dozen people digesting lunch, it's in your interest to be dynamic. If you project a series of slides with the lights out, the effect is guaranteed."

The problem lies essentially in the conception of the role and the missions of a trainer. Gilles A., a trainer primarily of managers, pursues the analysis:

> It's primarily the group that produces, that brings out meaning. It's not arrows, diagrams, circles, triangles. The tool sends you back to a question—where is the focus, on the speaker or the medium?—whether it involves teaching, influence, or persuasion. Is it the tool? Is it the speaker? If the speaker takes the central position, the tool can be used well. If the central place is left to the tool, it will seize it and the speaker will no longer be aware that the tool is managing the meeting. If the tool is in the center, the speaker is sending a clear message: he is letting the tool do the job. You measure the consequences when you're on the other side of the stage. On the pretext of being sure to transmit the message, a manager makes you swallow a series of slides. He reassures himself and you think he's hiding behind the tool. Managers see very clearly how the mistake happens. Once the tool contains the information, people think displaying it is all you need to do to transmit it.

The trainer steps aside, giving the medium the stage. He no longer bears messages or transmits meaning. The audience is subjected to a linear and single-minded discourse. Reception becomes passive, whereas the act of transmission requires interaction between speaker and audience, one feeding off the contributions of the other. The medium becomes the only focus of the exchange, and the pedagogical process is limited to the reading and reception of a long list of instructions.

PowerPoint fosters passive acceptance: individuals are asked to approve data on which they have expended no thought. The documents have been conceived and written beforehand in another context. The trainee is there only to take in and ratify a preestablished procedure that he will later have to reproduce. With PowerPoint, the trainee does not challenge himself and cannot discuss the content of his training. According to Florence, "PowerPoint tends to promote a lecture-style approach, with teachers who haven't mastered very much." Unlike what advertisements promoting the software suggest—emphasizing particularly the ease with which it makes anyone creative—the medium encourages a one-way discourse based on mastery and authority.

In addition to this lecturer-audience relationship often criticized by trainers, it also needs to be said that the trainer has to capture the attention of his listeners in order to be heard and understood. A PowerPoint presentation decreases attentiveness and provokes distraction. In short, the best medium for a training session is a trainer and a sheet of paper or a blackboard, enabling her to demonstrate in steps, to follow a sequence, to deploy an argument, to make corrections, and to retrace steps.

In a pedagogical situation, PowerPoint imposes technical and graphic constraints: formats, typographies, rules and norms imposed by companies, and logistical, computer, and visual arrangements that do not correspond to the requirements of an appropriate training program. The sequential constraint, the duty to follow a prescribed and immutable order regulated by the rhythm of the projection, is contrary to the principles of pedagogy. Again according to Florence:

> You can hardly escape from the expected path, digress, explore sidetracks, go forward or back, because that breaks the rhythm and might disconcert the trainees who have to make the double effort to follow the material presented and the way it is taught. In a "creativity" session, you're in a paradoxical command situation because you're asking them to be creative and at the same time

to follow tight frameworks, because PowerPoint sharply limits expression and imagination.

Some trainers demand *No PowerPoint*. Why? "Because," Gilles explains, "with these tools you're starting from the postulate that once the individual has had access to the concept, he has integrated, understood, retained, and memorized it. You assume that learning can take place in a linear, sequential way. But that's a complete illusion." In a pedagogical process, students memorize by association. With very simple messages written on sheets of paper and distributed at random on a wall, for example, trainees are faced with a sequence that enables them by association to read and create meaning. This kind of learning is impossible with PowerPoint. "Once the message has been heard, you want to remember it. You can backtrack, but that breaks up the sequence."

Many of these professional trainers criticize PowerPoint for its mechanical and disembodied aspect. The dynamics of learning depend on contact, gestures, feeling, and the process of association, whereas PowerPoint suppresses emotion, the affective aspect of the relationship between the trainer and his audience. When the trainer draws a diagram, the audience captures the intensity involved in making the gestures. There is a rational dimension: the spectator reproduces the diagram himself, the drawing, the curve; he writes at the same time as the trainer. A communion is thereby established, through the imitation of gestures, between the trainer and his audience who are all in the same time frame. With pre-written slides, a time lapse intervenes between the moment of production and the moment of presentation to the audience, the moment of decoding. With PowerPoint, the audience is at no point in a relation of identification, co-creation, or affective or cognitive interaction. The trainee is in attendance as a spectator and does not participate as an actor. His learning is shaky because he is not invested in it.

UNIVERSITY.PPT

These sets of questions associated with learning, pedagogical practice, and the influence of the software program are also being asked in schools and universities.

The new information and communication technologies made their entry onto American campuses in the first half of the 1990s. In 1995 a national survey of computer use in higher education (650 colleges and universities) found a 50 percent increase in the use of the new technologies in one year, including e-mail, office and multimedia software, and the Internet. Despite this progression, a gap persisted between the demand of students, who were very fond of these advances, which were starting to become part of their daily life, and the university, reputedly cautious about them. Nonetheless, from graduate economics departments to undergraduate colleges, about 80 percent of the teaching staff acknowledged that use of the Web would be indispensable within three years.

With the spread of new hardware and software, particularly PowerPoint, on campuses, came studies in specialized journals.[7] These rigorous and detailed studies relied on observations of large samples of students and attempted to answer very pragmatic questions: What is the pedagogical effectiveness of PowerPoint? And can it improve learning?

The studies were divided into two camps. One was rather indulgent and sought primarily to find ways of improving use of the software through commonsense recipes. The other had greater reservations about the effectiveness of PowerPoint but acknowledged that it was now difficult to do without it.

These two camps often overlapped, but with a division between disciplines. In hard-science departments, visual aids and transparencies were already common pedagogical devices. PowerPoint facilitated the design, production, and projection of graphs, diagrams, tables, and illustrations. The software was also well received in departments of economics, management, marketing, and communications. In the late 1990s, the attraction of these subjects for students and the novelty of the software probably had to do with its adoption.

But in other disciplines, it was a different story. David Farkas, professor of design at the University of Washington and incidentally fairly critical of the use of the software,[8] points out that the values of some academic communities may be in complete contradiction to the use of a software program of this type. In a department of communications, it seems normal for students to use PowerPoint in their preliminary exams or oral finals. But in the literature department next door, such a use of PowerPoint would seem incongruous:

> Recent publications by members of a scholarly community of ethnographers and geographers reveal a profound ambivalence toward PowerPoint as a means of reporting research results. The ambivalence arises, at least in part, because PowerPoint embodies corporate values and power. [A British geographer] asks: Does PowerPoint use "implicate geographers in the institutional power of Microsoft?"[9]

In disciplines like history, languages, literature, and philosophy, devoted to discursive and expository forms inherited from the history of their disciplines, PowerPoint is much less present.

Starting in 2003, criticism of the ubiquity of the program began to surface, along with skepticism about its real effectiveness for learning. Articles in the press played a role,[10] as well as the first monograph on PowerPoint, published by Edward Tufte in 2003 (see note 3 to the introduction).

In one of the first surveys of the literature on the subject, published in 2006, two communications professors, David Levasseur and J. Kanan Sawyer, made a rather radical observation: "The majority of extant studies have found no significant change in learning outcomes when instructors augment their lectures with computer-generated slides."[11] In the same year, two management professors, Russell Craig and Joel Amernic, deepened the analysis. They considered the dynamics of the pedagogical environment as well as the relationship between the presenter and the content presented. Although PowerPoint had been very widely adopted in management circles, they were surprised at the small number of authoritative studies of its effectiveness.

Those studies, conducted in the United States and England, usually consisted of comparing student outcomes in classes taught with and without PowerPoint. Others were based on the reporting of anecdotes. Most were conducted among populations that had experienced teaching before PowerPoint.

> In the main, the results reported in scholarly journal articles indicate that students like to be taught using PowerPoint (perhaps because of its novelty and the availability of printed handouts of PowerPoint slides) and think that PowerPoint presentations are entertaining, enhance clarity, and aid recall of subject matter. There is little consistent evidence, however, to show that teaching with PowerPoint leads to significantly better learning and significantly better grades than teaching by more conventional methods. A majority of studies shows that use of PowerPoint is not associated with a significant improvement in student grades.[12]

These studies establish that the penetration of PowerPoint is especially noteworthy in academic disciplines that prepare students for professions in which the software has a dominant presence. It is hardly surprising that specialized journals of communication, management, and accounting devote articles or even entire issues to good and bad uses of the software.[13] And these articles contain very few virulent criticisms, an indication of resignation in the face of a tool that has become ubiquitous.

And yet the Japanese Satoshi Sugahara and the Australian Gregory Boland conducted a study of an accounting class in order to compare student preferences and their academic performances. Their conclusion is not much of an argument in favor of the pedagogical effectiveness of the software or for its use in practical exercises:

> The preference of students for PowerPoint is inversely proportional to their final exam grades. And despite our enthusiasm about the use of PowerPoint in university accounting classes, it seems unlikely to lead to higher grades on exams. Moreover, if we consider exam results to be a measure of the degree of understanding, our results suggest that courses with PowerPoint are harmful to their learning.[14]

Most important, the study establishes the relative inability of students to summarize a course on the basis of a PowerPoint presentation compared to traditional note taking in a lecture course. And there was a specific result in the discipline of accounting: learning through PowerPoint—and more generally through the computer—prevents the development of basic accounting skills such as mental arithmetic.

This is another example of the deleterious effects of the passivity implicit in the use of PowerPoint, but also of the potential for distraction in the software and its decorative resources: "The frequent use of images and animation facilitated by PowerPoint may distract students from understanding the basic concepts of the course content."[15] In short, the effects initially designed to increase attentiveness—animation, sound effects, eye-catching images, and so on—actually weaken the concentration of the student audience and make them forget material.

Two professors at Delft University of Technology agree. They note that "it is striking that properties typical of PowerPoint are mainly mentioned as annoyances," and they think that PowerPoint encourages the teacher to serve "as a kind of stage-hand" for the device, and the device occupies all the audience's attention to the detriment of the teacher and what she is presenting.[16] Paradoxically, for some, the lecture course has recovered its pedagogical virtues: "Traditional lecture supporters mentioned the preference for good teacher-class interaction and their frustrations with PowerPoint . . . 'I gain more from lectures because I will pay attention to what is being said versus falling asleep to a boring PowerPoint presentation.'"[17]

The major weaknesses abetted by the tool are mentioned by the students themselves: the use of animation, illegible slides, illogical constructions, sloppy graphs, incoherent color schemes, and especially the speaker's bad practice of merely reading slides. Although PowerPoint may sometimes allow students to concentrate on the teacher's lecture, it takes away their ability to summarize or make outlines, and they end up remembering nothing but jargon. This effect can be all the more negative because some students think they are learning when they half doze in front of slides that are supposed to enable them to digest hours and hours of a course or whole chapters of a textbook without writing a single note.

One of the pitfalls of PowerPoint often mentioned by teachers is the gradual abandonment of note taking. Slides are usually available on Web sites where students get documents before or after class. For students, a good course is one that has PowerPoint backup.

The question of the relationship between teacher and students remains. To what extent does the program modify the pedagogical relation, the classroom space, the interaction and gestures of participants, the position of teacher and students, and so on?

First question: does the teacher or speaker disappear behind the device, or does he profit from it? The answer is banal: it depends on his talent. A good teacher will focus attention on his lecture, a bad one on the slides. Second question: what distance does PowerPoint impose between teacher and students? Answer: without PowerPoint, direct communication is favored, and exchanges are "more human, direct, less premeditated." With PowerPoint, the light is dimmed, and everyone tends to look at the screen, so there is no possibility of interaction with the teacher. The projection imposes attentiveness, calm, even somnolence. Slides are projected in the dark and establish their own necessity, barring any discussion of their status as true, half true, or false. The usual flow of words from speaker to audience is diverted: the teacher starts talking to the screen, not to the audience. All authority has thus devolved on the person presenting the slides, because she has mastered their pace and order of appearance and disappearance.

It has been noted that most teachers who use PowerPoint conceive of the role of educator as one-way transmission. They don't share knowledge, they deliver it. No work of construction or joint development is conducted. All that counts is the delivery of knowledge packaged into a few slides and bullet points. The student audience just has to watch the show presented to it instead of listening actively and really acquiring knowledge. As in the case of training, the pedagogical relation is deeply affected. The teacher no longer exercises his ascendancy solely through language or gesture as in a traditional class. He relies on projected images and gives up the relationship of sharing instituted by more participatory methods. The teacher often presents nothing but sets of summaries or instructions that students will have to follow and apply. He is no longer providing more or less objective data to help the students understand the world, but rather a toolbox designed to solve problems.

The unexpected paradox is that the program, presented as a modern pedagogical tool, seems to turn out in practice to be a tool in the service of a traditional pedagogy that "imposes an authoritarian presenter/audience relationship rather than facilitating a give-and-take exchange of ideas and information,"[18] and emphasizes the function of "transmission of knowledge" cherished by advocates of traditional teaching methods at the expense of everything else.

POWERPOINT ATTACKS THE HUMANITIES

"Facs: un rapport pour en finir avec 'la fabrique à chômeurs'" (Universities: a report to end the "manufacture of unemployment") was the evocative headline with which *Le Figaro* greeted the transmission on January 13, 2010, of the report of the Council for the Development of the Humanities and Social Sciences to the minister of higher education and research, Valérie Pécresse.[19] Established a year earlier, this committee was charged with presenting to the minister a view of the research and teaching issues in the humanities and social sciences and to suggest concrete actions to be taken. Chaired by Marie-Claude Maurel, director of studies at the École des Hautes Études en Sciences Sociales (EHESS), made up of eminent professors from various human and social sciences (HSS), the members of the council also included two business leaders, Franck Riboud of Danone and Serge Villepelet of PricewaterhouseCoopers France.

The report indicated a few avenues for improving the integration of HSS students into the world of work. In a chapter titled "Employability of students in human and social sciences," the committee challenged the accepted idea that these subjects "created unemployed people" but acknowledged that students of them were more likely to be hired in the public sector.[20] Although the report brought out the attraction of HSS students to teaching, it also noted that private companies were beginning to hire these "well-made minds," generalists who departed from the "usual profile of business schools or Anglo-Saxon programs."

In its selection of criteria for recruitment, the committee emphasized the skills required for HSS students to have a chance of being hired by private companies: sense of autonomy, ability to analyze and synthesize, general culture, attention to the human factor, all qualities that are not foreign to the values of neo-Taylorism. Candidates also should have "a real *capacity for expression*, written or oral" and be able to "present a question while captivating their audience." That teachers or future company managers should be able to present a question at a meeting does not seem inappropriate, but why should they "captivate" their audience? Why shouldn't they be satisfied with "persuading" their audience by deploying a well-constructed argument?

If captivating is the issue, familiarity with PowerPoint is a plus. Unsurprisingly, the ruling software program makes its entry on page 40 of the report, under the heading HSS and the PowerPoint Presentation.

Our discussions have included a cordial dialogue in which, whereas one of the two company heads on the committee, sitting as a qualified person, regrets the possible confinement of his managerial employees to the PowerPoint style of presentation, which might make them unable to prepare a long and organized presentation, another member of the council, a teacher-researcher, pointed out: "A good PowerPoint presentation is not an unstructured succession of pages unconnected with one another. In fact, the general organization of a PowerPoint presentation is an intricate exercise precisely because it involves reconciling the audience's perception of the underlying logic of the presentation with the brevity of each page. Further, the composition of the heading and the content of a PowerPoint page is a remarkable exercise in concision and clarity, because what is projected should not duplicate the longer phrases spoken simultaneously, nor distract the audience's attention from what is being said. Finally, PowerPoint provides great possibilities for using diagrams, graphs, maps, symbols, and the like. For all these reasons, graduates in the human and social sciences should acquire the skill to prepare PowerPoint files and that is one of the skills we should mention in our report." In any event, these two members of the council are arguing for the same thing: the rehabilitation of the art of rhetoric and therefore hiring university graduates in the humanities and social sciences.

This is the world turned upside down. A business leader attacks a tool that he knows is one of the pillars of contemporary business, while from the university comes a defense of the "dumbing-down" tool. The professor thinks HSS students "should acquire" this skill if they want to be hired by a company. HSS students should know how to "prepare PowerPoint files," which will at the same time make possible the "rehabilitation of the art of rhetoric." So it's skill in manipulating PowerPoint, not mastery of discourse, that enables us to evaluate the quality of the reasoning and the arguments of future employees. Once again, the medium replaces the content, the tool takes the place of thinking.

This promotion of PowerPoint in a 2010 report, in any event, demonstrates that the entry of the program into the French university system has been rather tentative in comparison to Anglo-Saxon campuses. Naturally, the first users were business and management schools and departments of management, accounting, and communication, especially in professional schools, thereby corroborating the usual French contrast between the university with a "theoretical" purpose and the often private *grandes écoles* for engineers and other specialists dedicated to "applied" disciplines.

Although slower, the intrusion of PowerPoint into public higher education was nonetheless confirmed in the early 2000s. Arnaud L., an assistant professor of economics now based in Berlin, started to use PowerPoint in 2002, first to prepare his classes and replace his outmoded and cumbersome transparencies, and later for presentations at conferences and seminars. Attendance at international conferences and the fact of having to speak English require the use of PowerPoint. It's an invaluable medium that "helps dissipate accent problems and keep track of the framework of the presentation." Generally speaking, international conferences now require speaking English and the use of slides, often asked for in advance. This forced adaptation to PowerPoint has also been encouraged by courses designed for foreign students.

PowerPoint seems to be primarily a helping device, a prompter in case of a memory lapse or a weakness in the demonstration. According to Martin S., who teaches at Paris Dauphine: "When I write a lecture, I detail the outline, the argument, the structure. It's written with an introduction, an outline that identifies the subject, why this outline, a definition of the theme, and the unfolding of the argument. PowerPoint is just a communication aid that makes my life easier, so I don't have to draw illegible diagrams or tables. It's a tool that provides support, assistance."

A new aspect of the spread of PowerPoint seems more problematic. More and more specialized schools (business, management, communication, and so on) now evaluate examinations on the basis of PowerPoint presentations. According to a management teacher: "In the case of presentations, I authorize students to rely on PowerPoint. But I never judge on the quality of slides but on their ability to formulate the question and organize their presentation. We know there are always students who are better orally than in writing. But their level of comfort can also indicate that they spent more time and worked harder on the subject." This account should be compared with the reservations expressed by some students in business and communications schools, who often complain about the many hours spent polishing their presentations. "We have ten minutes to formulate an issue, argue, answer a question. You have to be clear in your presentation, comfortable speaking, and rely on a presentation that has a few sparks," according to a masters student in communications. Students find themselves transformed into strategic advisers, advertisers, or HR consultants during an oral exam. They have to "sell" their presentation, or even themselves, because they will be judged on their ability to get their message across. The circle is complete, and the HSS elite of the French university system who worked for the minister can be satisfied: PowerPoint contamination is well and truly on the march in French higher education.[21]

FROM POWERPOINT TO THE INTERACTIVE WHITEBOARD: TOWARD A DIGITAL SCHOOL?

This trend is no doubt connected to a much larger process that has produced a profound change in educational models, a change that might make one fear that tools like PowerPoint will eventually also become part of secondary and even primary education.

The sociologist Christian Laval thinks that

> school is now subject to the general economic logic of competitiveness, in its goals, its political justification, its practical categories, its forms of organization. A new style of governing the school has taken hold which touches the heart of the teaching profession, directly affects pedagogical relationships, and changes the meaning of learning and the nature of teaching. It is governed by a system of competition and surveillance, a supposed guarantee of performance.[22]

There is indeed no reason why the school should not be subject to the same frameworks and constraints as society in general, that it should not use the same language and the same tools.

In the mid-1990s, the OECD launched the international assessment system PISA (Program for International Student Assessment), which compared the knowledge and skills of students in reading, mathematics, science, and problem solving, based on skill sets defined in the DeSeCo (Definition and Selection of Competencies) program. In 1997, the international organization considered the question of education in developed countries and its ability to deal with the environment and evolution of the contemporary world. A document explains the goals of the program:

Today's societies place challenging demands on individuals, who are confronted with complexity in many parts of their lives. What do these demands imply for key competencies that individuals need to acquire? Defining such competencies can improve assessments of how well prepared young people and adults are for life's challenges, as well as identify overarching goals for education systems and lifelong learning.[23]

The notion of competency is not limited to knowledge or skill. It includes a psychological and behavioral component: to communicate well, individuals have to possess linguistic knowledge, practical skills (they must know how to carry out a task), and interpersonal skills, the ability to adopt the proper attitude toward their interlocutors.[24] The DeSeCo program divides into three categories the competencies that individuals need to acquire if they are to "face the complex challenges of today's world": "Use tools interactively (e.g., language, technology)," "Interact in heterogeneous groups," and "Act autonomously."[25]

One cannot but be troubled by the resemblance between these three competencies and those required today by every HR director of a post-Fordist employee: mastery of tools (chiefly computers), ability to work in a group and autonomously, capacity to adapt to the requirements of a project. The competencies to be acquired in school on which the student will be assessed are the same as those required of the good employee. On the basis of this observation, the teacher and philosopher Angélique del Rey has developed a vigorous critique of this new educational doctrine adopted everywhere in the world:

It is hard to still believe the claim that the reason we had to define a "common core of knowledge and competencies" was to make possible, with a view toward the democratization of education, "success for all." For underlying the core are key competencies, a strategy for the development of "human resources," and behind that strategy the well known "theory of human capital" (man seen as a means) and a "new management of companies" with its logic of competition at all costs.[26]

Not satisfied with having instituted the same assessment standards in schools as in companies, the post-Fordist school system has also introduced all the tools of business. This transformation of education into a commodity goes back to the 1950s and 1960s in the United States, notably in Chicago, where research in human capital was conducted. From that point on, in the face of the instability of the world economy, companies began to incorporate human capital as an essential resource for their development. And when you say *capital*, you imply the ability to make it grow.

By 1962, the OECD had already enshrined the "notion of human capital as a factor of development, in addition to the factors of capital and labor." This step imposed on individuals the idea that they were in some sense the owners of a fund of knowledge and competencies that they had to foster and develop throughout their lives. This reification of human intelligence and accelerated individualization have profoundly modified social relations between employer and employee. Sociologists of work, no doubt for generous reasons (equality of opportunity, raising the level, and so on),[27] accelerated this change, leading to a new kind of management that measured labor power through competencies:

The new management constructs instruments to manipulate a worker confronted with the necessity of taking initiatives to resolve conflicts and problems that stand in the way of his competitiveness. Competencies are the basic concept of this instrumental analysis of the cognitive labor force. "Competency logic," as it is known, corresponds to a stage of personnel management in which the company strategically uses the worker's cognitive and emotional resources to increase his competitiveness.[28]

What connection does this change have with the school system? This logic of competencies fits into the framework of "lifelong learning" that has become in the 2000s a litany in international organizations, such as the OECD and the European Union.[29] This is an "instrumental conception of educational activities as a whole" that has largely inspired government educational policies in most developed countries. Education of children is directed toward employment, and its foundation stone is the company. "This conception has directly inspired the policies of recent decades that have placed employment concerns at the heart of the educational system, in different styles and with various degrees of intensity depending on the segments involved."[30]

With the law of 1971, continuing education was imposed on companies as a complementary educational mission. As a consequence, devotees of the market[31] accused the French educational system of not providing employers with enough young recruits with adequate competencies to become part of the company.

The pedagogical model of competencies represents perhaps the most eloquent example of this change of pedagogical perspective that has gradually penetrated the school system since the 1999 publication of the "Charte de programmes" (1992), a set of governing principles according to which the contents of teaching from primary school to *lycée* have to be redefined; in this document, the notion of competencies is constantly called upon.[32]

Gradually the educational policies put in place became focused on a logic of employment. Every individual was to be evaluated on the basis of the acquisition (or not) of competencies. And as Lucie Tanguy crisply notes, we moved "from an academic organization of degree courses to individual career paths" and "from education as a state concern to training as a matter of contracts."

In this framework, anticipating the "student/trainee," it seemed logical that PowerPoint would come into its own. Simultaneously an instrumental competency and a set of abilities corresponding to expectations—ability to communicate, to express oneself, to work in a group, and so on—the practice of PowerPoint could become a central element of this "new pedagogy" and its assessment methods.

Microsoft was not mistaken when it granted teachers providing their school's identification number free downloads of Office. Backed by the national education system, which encourages teachers to use it, the software has very "naturally" spread to secondary education. The use of slides has become a significant vector for learning and assessment in the educational world.

In many disciplines, classes are shaped by PowerPoint. There is a profusion of course templates on specialized Web sites and teachers' blogs.[33] Teachers exchange templates, illustrations, and so on. You can find complete presentations, aids for slide design for *collèges* and *lycées*: reading, math, natural sciences, from the French Revolution to romantic literature, from Darwin to the Bible, you gain access to complete sequences of downloadable PowerPoint courses.

It should be said that software use is more and more frequent at home and in the office. "Sometimes it's easier to use Word or PowerPoint for homework," says one parent, especially because adolescents, "digital natives," are born with a mobile phone at their ear and a keyboard at their fingertips. Even in *collège*, students prepare presentations with PowerPoint on computers at home. Senior *lycée* students can also design *travaux personnels encadrés* (supervised personal work) by copying and pasting materials collected on the Web.[34]

The intrusion of PowerPoint into schools might seem to be an epiphenomenon amid the technological arsenal that has invaded classrooms and playgrounds in recent years. New technologies at school include not only computers, educational software, the Internet, and software and media libraries. We also have to contend with "educational platforms," "digital workplaces," and "interactive whiteboards." The educational computer industry has a promising future.

The interactive whiteboard (IWB) or interactive digital board (IDB) is a device combining the advantages of a tactile screen with those of video projection:

> A veritable mural computer that makes it possible to write, mask, or display any kind of document: texts, images, sounds, videos; to correct an exercise or to question students individually to instantaneously assess the knowledge they have acquired on a given subject. . . . It introduces considerable changes of perspective in every phase of the teacher's work: conception and preparation, conduct of the class, individual attention, evaluation, reconstruction, review, and so on.[35]

The IWB, which is slated to replace the traditional blackboard in the coming years, represents the ideal medium for "powerpointing" the school, because it basically presents the same procedure and produces the same logic as Microsoft's leading software product.

Although there are various kinds of IWBs based on diverse

technologies, the principle is always the same: you can create, modify, manipulate, and present digital content directly on a large tactile display screen, with a finger, a stylus, or a remote.

Right now it is hard to measure the advantages and drawbacks of IWBs. "A survey by the Ministry of Education shows that 95 percent of teachers are satisfied with their use, and another survey by the European Commission of French teachers shows that they acknowledge the impact of these devices on student attention and motivation (88 percent for the IDB and 76.8 percent for the computer, all levels taken together)."[36]

The first studies are thus positive, as is often the case in the first phases of the implementation of new technologies: ease, functional aspect, comfort, novelty, playful character, dynamism, and the like are all elements fostering pedagogical use, particularly in the manipulation of multimedia documents for teachers and in attention and pleasure for students. Many Anglo-Saxon studies have also been enthusiastic,[37] although others point to "a risk of reinforcing teaching as transmission by lecture with a decrease in group work in classes with the device."[38]

With the proliferation of screens at school, are we not witnessing the gradual digitalization—and why not soon the virtualization—of all of education? It is in any event a very lucrative market for professionals. As one of the major suppliers to the French educational system, Emmanuel Pasquier, the general manager of Promethean, leader in IWB in France, has noted: "Eighty percent of IWBs are currently used in the educational sector. Promethean's customers represent more than 5,000 classes in about 200 mid-size or large cities (Limoges, Ploërmel, Levallois, Élancourt), departments (Allier, Cantal, Charente), and regions (Lorraine, Auvergne). The market is growing enormously: on average it doubles every two years and we have seen an acceleration in the last year, which is not limited to the French system." For this professional in educational computer technology, the future may well seem radiant: "The interactive whiteboard (IWB), the mobile classroom, and the digital workplace are the three winners in ICTE."[39]

This technological explosion in schools is the fruit of an underlying movement that has affected the educational world for the last ten years. In the 1990s, the Internet began to appear in secondary schools. In 1997, the Department of Scientific Information and New Technologies in the Ministry of Education considered that "the school system cannot remain aloof from these developments at the risk of producing students unequipped to deal with the information society." The European Union got involved in 1999 with the publication of a report, "e-Europe, an Information Society for All," made public at the 2000 Lisbon summit. The first of the ten propositions of the project was "Bring European youth into the digital era." The goal was well chosen: there was at the time strong growth in the computer market, which was able to create needs by regularly renewing its increasingly enticing and increasingly inexpensive offerings.

"Schools have to adapt to the challenges of information and communication technology. That is the purpose of the digital workplace, which provides a secure space." Thus begins the video presentation of the digital workplace on a Ministry of Education site dedicated to this new tool.[40] Was this just an awkwardness of expression? It is surprising to see a reversal of the ordinary logic that technology adapts to the school and not vice versa. In videos produced by the Caisse des Dépôts and local communities, the emphasis is on "competitiveness," "saving time," "economic development," and so on. One of the videos even speaks of the digital workplace as a "management tool" designed to communicate about school life.

Digital workplaces represent a spectacular breakthrough on

the path to the digitalization of classroom exchanges. Teachers often complain that attendance is low at meetings with parents, but now they will be able to communicate by computer. Digital workplaces are, in fact, a set of digital services made available to the educational community and accessible through any computer connected to the Internet.[41] It is a "virtual office" for the teacher and an "electronic school bag" for the students that permits access to the tools and content they need for their school activities. The services provided range from the management of school life (notebooks, grades, competency reports, control of absences and workspaces, and so on) to communication tools (instant messaging, forums, blogs, and so on), and provision to students by the teacher of digital resources. This digital environment, a school intranet,[42] will eventually make it possible to maintain continuous communication between the school and the outside world, like what now happens in most workplaces. So the teacher, the student, or the parent (if they have a computer) can be permanently connected on the digital workplace.

In 2003, the Ministry of Education established an overall plan for digital workplaces (Schéma Directeur des espaces numériques de travail, SDET) which outlined the strategy for implementing digital workplaces in schools at the regional level. At the beginning of the 2009–2010 school year, all regional academies, in partnership with the territorial communities, were joined in a digital workplace project at various stages, from preliminary study through experimentation to full implementation. Two thirds of the academies were in the implementation phase, including about half the departments and two thirds of the regions.[43]

In order to accelerate the movement, Education Minister Xavier Darcos engaged a committee under Jean Mounet, who presented a report a few months later. Jean Mounet is the managing director of Sopra Group, a major French computer engineering service company, and chairman of Syntec Informatique, an industry association of French computer companies and software publishers. The committee had only eight government members out of twenty-seven participants. As correctly noted by two teachers whose school is equipped with digital workplaces,

> this report is of major interest, to begin with because of the circumstances in which it was prepared. The economic interests of companies fixed the goals, the pace, the method, and the forms of development of the computerization of schools, down to advice about "communication" strategies to impose digital workplaces on all involved in school. It is also interesting because the strictly educational aspect of the transmission of knowledge is absent from a strategy that is essentially technical and economic. This strategy is a fairly typical example of the outsourcing to the private sector of functions and activities that had previously been completely a matter of public service. Public service has become de facto dependent on a both technical and commercial development of the tools that will determine its own operation and evolution. The school is becoming privatized: the sites where data about student education and the work of teachers are recorded and accessible are now governed by *private law*, not *public law*.[44]

The two teachers present a solid indictment of a tool that seems to them to have many more drawbacks than advantages. Not only has there been an introduction of commercial and marketing logic impelled by computer makers and project managers into the sanctuary of the school—the installation of a digital workplace is comparable to any other computer project—but also the digital stations seem to be ineffective in pedagogical terms.

In this connection, the teachers recall the conclusions of the report from the Mission e-Educ submitted to Xavier Darcos in 2008, which stated with respect to the impact of ICTE on student performance:

> Surveys were conducted in 2000, 2003, and 2006 in the framework of the Program for International Student Assessment (PISA) of the OECD (OECD 2003). . . . The best performances in mathematics as well as in reading were generally found among students who had an average use of computers. This observation suggests that excessive use of computers could have a negative impact on school performance.

No one questions the fact that the use of new technologies has changed pedagogical practices, that they have improved the atmosphere in classes. But more problematic, aside from the pedagogical aspect, seems to be the economic and social question, in particular mere access to computers, which is far from universal. In its 2008 study of the level of household computer ownership, the Centre de Recherche pour l'Étude et l'Observation des Conditions de Vie (CREDOC) showed that "two thirds of the French population has least one computer at home (66 percent), and 17 percent even have several."[45] Whereas more than 90 percent of upper-level households are well supplied, only 61 percent of workers are. This suggests that for almost one child of a worker out of ten, the paperless class is not for tomorrow, that the virtual school will leave them by the roadside. The two teachers also discuss the way digital workplaces call into question their own profession in the sense of dematerializing exchanges, a gradual obliteration of the time and space of the school, which is becoming a school "without walls." Then there's the "Big Brother" aspect of these exchanges, which will eventually make it possible to record and store information on students and their parents, transferable to any government department beyond the education service if the need arises. In this world of control, evaluation, and performance from early childhood,[46] some teachers have trouble recognizing themselves:

> The injunction to use digital tools and the fact they will soon be obligatory reveal a purely bureaucratic logic. And this type of logic, "from the top down," based on a lack of understanding of current teacher practices, is seldom a factor for success. The digital workplace, in a logic of management, precisely redefines the teaching profession "from above" by prescribing gestures and tasks in an almost Taylorist way.[47]

All international organizations, from the OECD to the European Union, have decreed that education is above all designed to enable children to acquire knowledge, to learn how to learn and understand. But it also has to train informed consumers, versatile workers, and compassionate administrators. The school has to equip its students with effective aptitudes and attitudes, has to shape behavior and provide the toolbox. In a sense it has to turn all those blond heads into resources usable as future needs and projects will require.

In this context, knowledge becomes a product, a service to consume, purchase, evaluate, and display. Students will no longer judge the value of their teachers by their lectures but by the quality of their slides or the show that goes along with them. They themselves will be judged on their ability to give a presentation in ten slides in ten minutes—speaking ability, ability to summarize, strength of conviction—in short, on their ability to sell themselves and to sell their skills and, incidentally, their knowledge.

Now that many exams are in multiple-choice form and the written essay is an exercise falling into disuse, it is hard not to imagine that in a few years, in the endless race and demand to exhibit oneself, exam rooms will be changed into auditoriums or theaters where every student will have to give a carefully prepared show—always form rather than content—so that the performance will get the greatest number of points possible. A presentation will have become an audition; the exam, a casting call.

CONCLUSION:
THE HIDDEN PERVERSITY
OF A SOFTWARE PROGRAM

PowerPoint is both a ubiquitous tool and a powerful medium, but it tends to promote use of an impoverished, standardized, and depersonalized language. The use of graphs and images is random and often useless, if not deceptive. The system it puts on stage makes any presentation resemble a "huge accumulation of spectacle," in the words of Guy Debord.

In twenty years, the program has also become the favored medium for a certain ideology, which prefers efficient action to reflection, rationalization to reason, and computer modeling to inspiration. This ideology, which the sociologist Vincent de Gaulejac calls "managerial" (*gestionnaire*), has become a system of thought with procedures and styles of representation that imbue many sectors of activity.

FROM THE "MANAGERIAL" PARADIGM TO COMPANY Y

Adulated in the 1980s, the model of the company—its management and organization—became the promised land of individual success and collective effectiveness. Confronted with hyperconsumption, globalization, and the demand for short-term profit, in the 1990s organizations had to change their language and the nature of relations among their employees. Organizations became "lighter" "flexible," and "horizontal." The new tools speeded up exchanges and at the same time made them fleeting, ephemeral, even incoherent. Communication became normalized, formalized, standardized. The "project" became the alpha and omega of any work in common. The new information and communication technologies blurred the boundaries between public and private.

The company became the site of all professional and especially personal adventures. According to the magazine *Enjeux–Les Échos*, the company of tomorrow, "communicating and global, will also be creative and responsible. . . . Pioneers are already clearing the ground, influenced by generation Y, otherwise known as 'digital natives.'"[1] This "company Y" will be "fun" and "cool," will not hesitate to promote itself with greenwashing[2] campaigns and increased diversity to become a "best workplace"[3] and attract "high-potential" employees.

This perpetual change hardly stopped at the company's gates and is in the process of affecting all areas of human activity. It is also cognitive and even anthropological.[4] This "service capitalism" has put in place relational technologies[5] that equip "all areas of human existence with objects of constant and systematic control of attention and behavior."[6]

In this universe of immediacy and control, the individual has to submit or resign. Making a place for yourself in hyperindustrial society means abiding by a certain number of constraints: you have to be able to manage your fate like a series of personal projects by strengthening your professional "competencies" under the seal of "performance" and "autonomy," by being "innovative," "creative," and "always listening," to be able to "adapt." You also have to be able to sell yourself. The command to communicate is a foundation of our society. Exhibitionism and fiction about the self have become required exercises for individuals in search of identity and values.

Profoundly narcissistic, this model of the individual is focused solely on the satisfaction of his desires and considers his life only by the measure of his rights and his interest. But he wants to be integrated into normative frameworks to the extent that he deems them in harmony with the dominant model and thinks they will enable him to succeed. He is always present but irresponsible, always connected but never involved. His only values are those that enable him to "fulfill himself" and "develop personally," with no long-term project. He must be able to evaluate himself in order to respond to a situation of perpetual competition. In a word, entirely taken in hand by the technical-economic world, he has the illusion of autonomy, although he has lost all initiative.

POWERPOINT, A PARADOXICAL TOOL

PowerPoint is an ideal tool for staging both aspirations and resignation. By its nature and form, the software program is the perfect transmitter for this new organizational ecology, because it contains the same collection of paradoxes as those borne by an individual who has to stick to the middle of the road, on a knife edge, and is expected to adjust his desires to his restricted circumstances.

PowerPoint permits perpetual oscillation between reason and fiction, between seriousness and charm, between the illusion of freedom and the reality of constraint. It appears to foster the individual's creative energy, although it limits her expression and neutralizes her language. The individual clothes herself with the illusion of autonomy and freedom in a world that enforces

conformity in her actions and apathy in her speech, transforming her existence without any real participation from her.

Microsoft's leading software program has catalyzed all the
mirages around which early twenty-first-century society has
shaped itself. Focused on the short term, its use is quick and inexpensive; it provides a simplified and fragmented vision, so as to
be accessible and reproducible; it produces spectacular effects to
attract the audience; and it is minimalist to elude criticism.

PowerPoint carries perversity to the extreme of giving the
illusion of bringing together usefulness and pleasure. It allies
propaganda with illusion, the new universal rules of our show-
business world. It makes it possible to favor the object over the
subject, the container over the thing contained, form over content, and medium over message. We are reminded of the warnings issued by the Canadian sociologist Marshall McLuhan and
the often perspicacious denunciations of the French situationist
Guy Debord.

The last and not least important paradox is that whereas the
mastery and use of PowerPoint are now widespread and un-
avoidable, according to all the experts, the program is often ridi-
culed. Does everyone privately sense the perversity of a tool that
stimulates the mind while simultaneously constraining it, that
requires us to create, *commands* us to invent?

RESISTING THE POWERPOINTING OF THE WORLD

"With iPods and iPads; and Xboxes and PlayStations . . . information becomes a distraction, a diversion, a form of entertainment, rather than a tool of empowerment, rather than the means
of emancipation." President Barack Obama did not hesitate to
express his worry in his commencement address at Hampton
University in Virginia on May 9, 2010. Coming from a "President

Y" who had been so skillful in using the latest discoveries of digital communication, this cautious critique might make one smile. However, we have come far from the technological euphoria of the last two decades, whose high priests were Steve Jobs and Al Gore. Although we have definitively entered the information society, or the knowledge society, or the world of cognitive capitalism, adaptation does not need to mean submission.

It is time to reinvent the right to resist and to subscribe to the advice of two management experts who propose to "reintroduce the right to not use PowerPoint for a presentation."[7] Some company heads have shown that kind of boldness in the past, among them Scott McNealy, the charismatic CEO of Sun Microsystems, who banned PowerPoint from his company in 1997, because he found that "it clogged disks, bandwidth, and brains."

It is especially brains that have to be protected from contamination, because the "grammar" of PowerPoint, in a kind of boomerang effect, has begun to infiltrate the very domains from which it drew its inspiration, as though the pupil had surpassed the master. Ads often take the form of slides; evening television news anchors often present one or another government reform with a plethora of screens modeled on PowerPoint presentations. In everyday private and professional life, e-mail servers around the world are clogged with documentary, comic, or other ppt files downloaded from hundreds of specialized Web sites. Weddings, births, christenings, birthdays all produce slide shows. It would be hard to deny that there is now a PowerPoint style of telling stories, from the Bible to May 1968. PowerPoint is simultaneously a language, a narrative form, and a show.

So does PowerPoint really make us stupid? With this provocative comment, General James Mattis was trying to warn against a kind of blind systematization, common in the military, that impels execution without thought. Although it may not make us stupid, there is no doubt that PowerPoint, like many other media, helps to make the world illiterate and contributes to the abandonment of critical thinking, to blind acceptance, to a new form of voluntary servitude. One of the aims of this book is to warn against the "PowerPointing" of minds. It is as though, subjected to the battering of the contemporary model of society, everyone had been forced, out of a concern for efficiency (always!) and in conformity to the dominant mode of thinking, to abandon any capacity to reason, to discuss, and to criticize; as though, after all, we could persuade with five slogans and two pictures—as though we had all become children again.

NOTES

INTRODUCTION

1. Elisabeth Bumiller, "We Have Met the Enemy and He Is PowerPoint," *New York Times*, April 26, 2010.

2. Ian Parker, "Absolute PowerPoint: Can a Software Package Edit Our Thoughts?" *New Yorker*, May 28, 2001.

3. Edward Tufte, *The Cognitive Style of PowerPoint: Pitching Out Corrupts Within*, 2nd ed. (Cheshire, CT: Graphics Press, 2006).

4. Ibid., 4 (emphasis in original).

1. THE INVENTION OF A UNIVERSAL MEDIUM

1. See JoAnne Yates, *Control Through Communication: The Rise of System in American Management* (Baltimore: Johns Hopkins University Press, 1989).

2. Alfred D. Chandler Jr., *The Visible Hand: The Managerial Revolution in American Business* (Cambridge, MA: Belknap Press Harvard University Press, 1977).

3. Organizations by "matrix" or "network" are contemporary variants.

4. Also known as I.E. DuPont de Nemours, this company,

established in the United States in 1802, became a global giant in chemistry and plastics in the twentieth century following the invention of nylon in its laboratories in 1935. With branches today in seventy countries and sixty thousand employees, the company had revenues of more than $30 billion in 2008.

5. See JoAnne Yates, "Graphs as a Managerial Tool: A Case Study of DuPont's Use of Graphs in the Early Twentieth Century," *Journal of Business Communication* 22, no. 1 (1985): 5–33.

6. JoAnne Yates and Wanda Orlikowski, "The PowerPoint Presentation and Its Corollaries: How Genres Shape Communicative Action in Organizations," in *Communicative Practices in Workplaces and the Professions: Cultural Perspectives on the Regulation of Discourse and Organizations*, ed. Mark Zachry and Charlotte Thralls (Amityville, NY: Baywood, 2007), 73.

7. Willard C. Brinton, *Graphic Methods for Presenting Facts* (New York: Engineering Magazine Co., 1914).

8. Large-format pads of paperboard set on a standing easel, generally written on with markers. This system is still very common in training programs and in business.

9. *A Century of Innovation: The 3M Story*, 57. A pdf file of this document can be downloaded from the company's Web site.

10. The expression *war room* has penetrated into the world of politics. In 1993, a documentary by Chris Hegedus and D.A. Pennebaker, *The War Room*, showed the operations of Bill Clinton's war room during the 1992 presidential campaign.

11. *Century of Innovation*, 58.

12. Some American police procedural films recall the use of these projections in investigations: for example, the scenes in Steven Spielberg's *Catch Me If You Can* (2002) in which FBI agent Carl Hanratty (Tom Hanks) projects visual presentations detailing the different types of falsification used by the criminal Frank Abagnale Jr. (Leonardo Di Caprio).

13. Letraset is a famous brand of dry transfer characters: printed

in sheets of different formats, the characters can be transferred one by one onto any surface by rubbing.

14. Ian Parker, "Absolute PowerPoint: Can a Software Package Edit Our Thoughts?" *New Yorker*, May 28, 2001.

15. Michel Volle, *De l'Informatique: Savoir vivre avec l'automate* (Paris: Economica, 2006), 72.

16. This late startup was a decisive factor in the loss of hegemony by a company that then dominated the world computer market, a market that was profoundly destabilized by the microcomputer.

17. Following Moore's famous law. The co-founder of Intel, Gordon Moore, predicted in 1965 that in light of the performance of electronic components—from transistors to microprocessors—the power of computers would double every year for at least ten years.

18. Éric Verdier, *La Bureautique* (Paris: La Découverte, 1983), 89.

19. New managerial "concepts" that were in vogue in the 1970s under the influence of gurus appointed by major American consulting firms like McKinsey and Boston Consulting Group (see below).

20. Norbert Alter, *La Bureautique dans l'entreprise*, 2nd ed. (Paris: L'Harmattan, 2005), 12.

21. Robert Reich, *The Work of Nations* (New York: Knopf, 1991).

22. Alter, *La Bureautique dans l'entreprise*, 68.

23. American manufacturer of projectors, notably of the ancestors of video projectors. In the 1980s, a Barco was a synonym for overhead projector.

24. Considered the ancestor of PowerPoint for Macintosh, it made it possible to create slide shows.

25. The least expensive on the market today produce more than 2,000 lumens and weigh less than six pounds.

26. Gaskins created a self-promoting blog in 2007 on the

occasion of the twentieth anniversary of the creation of Power-Point, www.robertgaskins.com. Quotations from Gaskins come from that site.

27. Volle, *De l'Informatique*, 105.

28. Parker, "Absolute PowerPoint."

29. The complete document is available on Gaskins's Web site. It demonstrates a certain sense of foresight.

30. Founded in 1886 by the accountant William Seward Burroughs, who invented the first adding machine. In 1962, Burroughs was the world's third largest producer of computers.

31. See his authoritative Web site www.concertina.com, which presents the work of eminent scholars and collections of historical documents. Gaskins has been an honorary life member of the International Concertina Association since 2005.

32. Parker, "Absolute PowerPoint."

33. Ibid.

34. Gaskins, "PowerPoint at 20: Back to Basics," *Communications of the ACM* 50, no. 12 (December 2007).

35. Ibid.

2. ANOTHER WAY OF WORKING

1. Used to describe a company with a "vertical" structure, in which each sector operates according to its own organization and has few connections to other departments. This is true, for example, of companies handling several lines of autonomous products, each with its own computer system, human resources management, advertising, and so on.

2. Today, administrative positions require, in addition to specific skills, knowledge of computer programs, even Web design and project management.

3. In 1975, slightly more than half the working population (52.9 percent) was employed in the service sector. In 1993, the

number reached almost 70 percent. In 2007, the French National Institute of Statistics and Economic Studies (INSEE) estimated the numbers working in services at 15 million, or 75 percent of the working population. Services are the largest employment sector in Germany, with nearly 28 million employees (72.4 percent). Services occupy 80 percent of the American working population and 72 percent in Japan. In Brazil, India, and China, the service sector employs respectively 64, 53, and 32 percent of the working population.

4. On this subject, see the remarkable book by Delphine Gardey, *Écrire, calculer, classer: Comment une révolution de papier a transformé les sociétés contemporaines 1800–1940* (Paris: La Découverte, 2008).

5. Many memoirs of stultifying work were published at the time, including the painful account by Robert Linhart, *The Assembly Line*, trans. Margaret Crosland (Amherst: University of Massachusetts Press, 1981), a first-person narrative by a graduate of the École Normale Supérieure, a Maoist militant who had taken a job in a suburban Paris factory.

6. Michel Lallement, *Le Travail: Une sociologie contemporaine* (Paris: Gallimard, 2007), 200.

7. This return to favor of the human factor is often attributed to the managerial current derived from the thinking of the human relations school of management created after the 1929 crash as a critique of Taylorism. This school sought to restore the individual to the center of the company's activities. Its best known representatives are Elton Mayo and Abraham Maslow.

8. According to standard X50-115; see Gilles Garel, *Le Management de projet* (Paris: La Découverte, 2003), 14.

9. Luc Boltanski and Ève Chiapello, *The New Spirit of Capitalism*, trans. Gregory Elliott (London: Verso, 2005).

10. Luc Boltanski, "Les changements actuels du capitalisme et la culture du projet," *Cosmopolitiques* 22 (June 12, 2006).

11. Boltanski and Chiapello, *New Spirit of Capitalism*, 98.

12. Michèle Lacoste, "Peut-on travailler sans communiquer?" in *Langage et travail: Communication, cognition, action*, ed. Annie Borzeux and Béatrice Fraenkel (Paris: CNRS Éditions, 2005).

13. Ibid., 51.

14. Ibid., 24.

15. Gérald Gaglio, "Faire des présentations, c'est travailler, mais comment? Diapositives numériques et chaîne d'activités dans des services marketing," *Activités* 6, no. 1 (April 2009): 115.

16. JoAnne Yates, "Genre Systems: Structuring Interaction through Communicative Norms," *Journal of Business Communication* 39, no. 1 (2002): 13–35.

17. A common term in management by project circles and beyond: "Deliverables are documents making possible the traceability of the project, communication with all participants, and the contractualization of relations between the participants in the project" (http://blog.lavoixduprojet.fr). Every assignment, every job today has its share of deliverables at its conclusion. The deliverable is even one of the principal exchange values—along with cost and deadline—that make it possible to measure the quality of a service provided.

18. In December 2009, there were 29,505 manuals on PowerPoint listed on Amazon.com, as well as 17,388 training manuals on the running of meetings.

19. Gaglio, "Faire des présentations, c'est travailler, mais comment?"

20. According to the terminology of JoAnne Yates and Wanda Orlikowski, who have devoted many articles to the subject and more generally to communication in companies.

21. Boltanski and Chiapello, *New Spirit of Capitalism*, 114.

22. See Cécile Tardy, Yves Jeanneret, and Julien Hamard, "L'empreinte sociale d'un outil d'écriture: PowerPoint chez les consultants," in *L'Écriture des médias informatisés—espaces de pratiques*, ed. Tardy and Jeanneret (Paris: Hermès Lavoisier, 2007), 141–71.

23. This development was analyzed remarkably well by the American sociologist and historian Christopher Lasch in *The Culture of Narcissism* (New York: W.W. Norton, 1979).

24. See Tardy, Jeanneret, and Hamard, "L'empreinte sociale d'un outil d'écriture," 156.

25. Some sociologists believe that contemporary society is "ill with time" and that we are now living under a tyrannical reign of urgency, the immediate, and the instant. See Nicole Aubert, *Le Culte de l'urgence* (Paris: Flammarion, 2003).

26. Valérie Beaudouin, "PowerPoint: le lit de Procuste revisité," *Social Science Information* 47 (2008): 383.

27. Boltanski and Chiapello, *New Spirit of Capitalism*, 80.

28. Created by the anthropologist Gregory Bateson, the notion of double bind refers to the insoluble relation between two contradictory constraints: "the obligation of each one containing the prohibition of the other." One of the most notorious examples in communication is the injunction "Be spontaneous!" Some psychologists believe this phenomenon may be the source of certain forms of schizophrenia.

29. On this subject, see Michela Marzano, *Extension du domaine de la manipulation: De l'entreprise à la vie privée* (Paris: Grasset, 2008).

3. BULLET-POINT RHETORIC

1. Such as Doug Lowe, *PowerPoint 2010 for Dummies* (Indianapolis: Wiley, 2010). Experts like Nancy Duarte, Garr Reynolds, and Guy Kawasaki have taken positions in the lucrative market for trendy guides designed to make slide shows sexier.

2. Presentation of the merger of two asset managers in 2009.

3. David Farkas, "Managing Three Mediation Effects That Influence PowerPoint Deck Authoring," *Technical Communication* 56, no. 1 (February 2009), 1–11.

4. Bernard Thiry, "Radiographie du langage de l'économie,"

La Banque des Mots 69 (2005): 111–21. All the tricks of this language are taught in the very official École de Guerre Économique in the seventh arrondissement of Paris, European affiliate of a famous American management school. See www.ege.fr.

5. A simplified version of English, using only the most common words and expressions. To learn how to speak globish, see www.globish.com.

6. Roberte Tomassone, *Pour enseigner la grammaire* (Paris: Delagrave, 1996), 234.

7. Ibid., 235.

8. See Claude Hagège, *Le Français et les siècles* (Paris: Odile Jacob, 1987).

9. On this subject, see, for example, Dominique Maingueneau, *Analyser les textes de communication* (Paris: Nathan, 2000), 166.

10. Alain Frontier, *La Grammaire du français* (Paris: Belin, 1997), 611.

11. Win-win is an essential notion in Newspeak and the kind of relationship to be fostered with associates, clients, suppliers, partners, and so on.

12. The reference is also, of course, to munitions.

13. Jack Goody, *The Domestication of the Savage Mind* (Cambridge: Cambridge University Press), 75.

14. Ibid., 80.

15. Ibid., 81.

16. Ibid., 103.

17. The term *literacy* is used to differentiate societies with a written culture from societies, often called primitive, with an oral culture.

18. Rafi Haladjian, "Devenez beau, riche et intelligent avec PowerPoint, Excel et Word," 2003, accessible at http://pauillac .inria.fr/~weis/info/haladjian.pdf, 9.

19. Biblical slide shows available at http://www.panorama -bible.ch.

20. Edward Tufte, *The Cognitive Style of PowerPoint: Pitching Out Corrupts Within*, 2nd ed. (Cheshire, CT: Graphics Press, 2006), 16.

21. Gordon Shaw, Robert Brown, and Philip Bromley, "Strategic Stories: How 3M Is Rewriting Business Planning," *Harvard Business Review* 76 (May–June 1998), 41.

22. Tufte, *Cognitive Style of PowerPoint*, 10–11.

23. Columbia Accident Investigation Board, *Final Report*, http:// caib.nasa.gov/news/report/pdf/vol1/full/caib_report_volume1.pdf, vol. 1, p. 191.

24. Edward Bernays, *Propaganda* (1928; Brooklyn, NY: Ig Publishing, 2005), 52.

25. Olivier Reboul, *Introduction à la rhétorique: Théorie et pratique* (Paris: PUF, 1998), 56–59.

26. Known as autotelic utterances: "closed to any real argumentative linkage and to any interaction, making up an argument in themselves." Jean-Michel Adam and Marc Bonhomme eds., *L'Argumentation publicitaire* (Paris: Armand Colin, 2007), 148.

27. Éric Hazan, *LQR: La propagande au quotidien* (Paris: Raisons d'agir, 2006), 40.

28. Philippe Forest and Gérard Conio, *Dictionnaire fondamental du français littéraire* (Paris: Bordas, 1993), 70.

29. Taken at random from several institutional presentations in 2008 and 2009.

30. The term *asyndetic parataxis* is also used to describe propositions that are juxtaposed with no indication of connections.

31. Michèle Aquien and Georges Molinié, "Euphémisme," *Dictionnaire de Rhétorique et de Poétique* (Paris: Livre de Poche, 1999).

32. Slides 20 and 21 in the 2004 report, April 26, 2005.

33. Slide 9 of the presentation.

34. It should be noted that one of PowerPoint's animated effects is the imitation of a typewriter's printing.

35. See www.definitions-marketing.com.

4. FROM OBFUSCATION TO FALSIFICATION

1. Claude Cossette, *Les Images démaquillés: Approche scientifique de la communication par l'image* (Québec: Riguil, 1983). Some chapters of this work are available at http://www.ulaval.ca.

2. Raphaël Lellouche, *Théorie de l'écran*, available at http://testconso.typepad.com/theorieecran.pdf. An old text that still has surprising predictive power.

3. Notably in the theories of Leon Battista Alberti (1404–1472), writer, philosopher, and theorist of mathematical perspective.

4. Thierry Chancogne, Course on the technology of communication and analysis of the image, available at http://lyc58-colas.ac-dijon.fr.

5. Christian Morel, *L'Enfer de l'information ordinaire* (Paris: Gallimard, 2007).

6. Ibid., 124.

7. Gestalt theory has proposed a number of laws. The law of good form: a group of formless parts tends to be perceived as a simple, symmetrical, stable, form. The law of proximity: we group together first the points that are closest to one another. The law of resemblance: elements of the same form or the same size will be more easily perceived as belonging to a single figure. The law of good continuity: we tend to continue an incomplete form along rational lines. The law of closure: a closed form is more easily identified as a figure than an open form. And the law of common outcome: parts in movement following the same trajectory are perceived as being part of the same form.

8. According to the well-known law of George Miller, published in "The Magical Number Seven," *Psychological Review* 63, no. 2 (1956): 81–97.

9. Dan Sperber and Deirdre Wilson, *Relevance: Communication and Cognition* (Cambridge, MA: Harvard University Press, 1986).

10. See http://thinkoutsidetheslide.com.

11. The author remarks that these 2007 results correspond to those of a 2003 survey, demonstrating that the use of PowerPoint changed little in four years.

12. Many presentations of this kind were available on the Web throughout the year 2009. One might note in passing the general inability to develop consistency in elements of the presentations, even in the very name of the virus, which changed several times before it was stamped with the code name H1N1.

13. Presentations viewed (a dozen) were of various lengths, from fifteen to eighty slides.

14. Especially on YouTube, where you can see videos by Doug Jefferys, Tim Lee, and the excellent Don McMillan.

15. See http://blog.guykawasaki.com.

16. Jacques Bertin, "La Graphique," *Communications* 15 (1970), 169 (a brief introduction to the discipline he created, graphic communication, about which he wrote a treatise: *Semiology of Graphics*, trans. William J. Berg [Redlands, CA: ESRI Press, 2011]).

17. Which implies a single meaning, unlike words, music, or images, which are polysemic.

18. The early 1980s were prolific in graphic analysis, particularly in the United States, as Stephen Kosslyn observes in a critique of five books published in 1985, including works by Tufte and Bertin: Stephen Kosslyn, "Graphics and Human Information Processing," *Journal of the American Statistical Association* 80, no. 391 (1985): 499–512.

19. His three most famous books, which he published himself for reasons of graphic precision, are *The Visual Display of Quantitative Information* (1983), *Envisioning Information* (1990), and *Visual Explanation* (1997), all published by Graphics Press, Cheshire, CT.

20. Tufte comments ironically on the barrels, gas pumps, and

derricks widely used as illustrative devices in American magazines during the oil shocks of 1973 and 1979.

21. The literature in England and America on this subject has been plentiful in the last twenty years. See in particular three papers by Vivien Beattie and Michael J. Jones: "A Six-Country Comparison of the Use of Graphs in Annual Reports," *International Journal of Accounting* 36, no. 2 (2001): 195–222; "A Comparative Study of the Use of Financial Graphs in the Corporate Annual Reports of Major U.S. and U.K. Companies," *Journal of International Financial Management and Accounting* 8, no. 1 (1997): 33–68; and "Australian Financial Graphs: An Empirical Study," *Abacus* 35, no. 1 (1999): 46–76.

22. Éric Maton, "Une analyse des diagrammes presents dans les rapports annuels des grandes enterprises françaises en 1980, 1990 et 2001," *Entreprises et Histoire* 44 (2006): 67.

23. Auditing firms, including Deloitte and Ernst & Young, had, it seems, made suggestions in this regard in 1995.

24. Ibid., 72.

25. Ibid., 83.

26. Ian Parker, "Absolute PowerPoint: Can a Software Package Edit Our Thoughts?" *New Yorker*, May 28, 2001.

27. The form was suggested to Belleville by her college roommate.

28. Mireille Betrancourt, Julie Bauer-Morrison, and Barbara Tversky, "Les animations sont-elles vraiment plus efficaces?" *Revue d'intelligence artificielle* 14, no. 1–2 (2000): 149–66.

5. A TOTAL SPECTACLE

1. Gérald Gaglio, "Faire des présentations," *Activités* 6, no. 1 (April 2009): 116.

2. Ibid., 119.

3. Ibid., 125.

4. See Caroline Datchary, "Prendre au sérieux la question de la dispersion au travail," *Réseaux* 125, no. 3 (2004).

5. Michael Flocker, *Death by PowerPoint: A Modern Office Survival Guide* (Cambridge, MA: Da Capo Press, 2006).

6. Valérie Beaudoin, "PowerPoint: le lit de Procruste revisité," *Social Science Information* 47 (2008): 378.

7. Ibid., 379–84.

8. Cécile Tardy, Yves Jeanneret, and Julien Hamard, "L'empreinte sociale d'un outil d'écriture: PowerPoint chez les consultants," in *L'Écriture des médias informatisés—espaces de pratiques*, ed. Tardy and Jeanneret (Paris: Hermès Lavoisier, 2007), 141–71.

9. Beaudoin, "PowerPoint," 379.

10. Ibid., 380–81.

11. Knoblauch looked at the use of the pointer—a small device that enables the speaker to create a point of light or a red arrow to indicate a particular point or area of a slide—in various PowerPoint presentations and at its interactions with the audience.

12. Hubert Knoblauch, "The Performance of Knowledge: Pointing and Knowledge in PowerPoint Presentations," *Cultural Sociology* 2, no. 1 (2008): 75–97.

13. What Tardy, Jeanneret, and Hamard call a "theater of expertise."

14. Respectively, software for retouching or creating images, creating Web sites, publishing (press), and animating images. Since then, the panoply has grown considerably richer.

15. A hit of the time that was used in the soundtrack of one of the most successful American horror movies, *The Exorcist*, by William Friedkin.

16. Steve Notes is a play on Apple's presentation software, Keynotes.

17. The studio that invented computer-generated animation; Steve Jobs bought Pixar in 1986 and sold it to Disney twenty years later.

18. Meaning it can't run anything but Apple software. One of the major criticisms of Apple is that the Mac is being completely closed to programs that run under other operating systems, primarily Microsoft Windows.

19. Jobs displays, for example, the percentage of users among creative artists, the press, advertisers, and Web designers, primary users and recommenders of the brand: 80 percent for the press, advertising professionals, and graphic artists, 64 percent for Web designers at the time.

20. With Microsoft holding a decisive and long-lasting lead in this market, the conflict between the two brands has been violent and passionate, punctuated by a few legal battles. Apple frequently accuses Gates's company of having plundered it. Incidentally, it is said that Apple has recently done its own plundering in mobile phone technology.

21. Examples: Alan Kay, one of the pioneers of the personal computer: "People who are really serious about software should make their own hardware"; Wayne Gretzky, the hockey player: "I skate to where the puck is going to be, not where it has been."

22. "Touch your music," "Your life in your pocket," and so on.

23. Even though the community, the press, and computer professionals were already aware of the new products.

24. Because Americans cannot imagine a good story without bad guys against whom the good guys have to fight, Apple has found villains to match it: IBM and Microsoft. The idea of fighting a common enemy is very potent and makes it possible to transform every customer into a promoter of the brand.

25. With the help of Nancy Duarte, a prominent American expert in presentations.

26. The festival guide promoted the documentary as a "gripping story" and "a visually mesmerizing presentation" that is "activist cinema at its very best." William Booth, *Washington Post*, January 26, 2006.

27. William Booth's ironic description, ibid.

28. Alex Steffen, "Interview: Davis Guggenheim and *An Incon-venient Truth*," May 4, 2006, www.worldchanging.com/archives/004388.html.

29. See, for example, an article by the business strategy consulting firm Norelli & Company: www.norelli.com.

30. David Stark and Verena Paravel, "PowerPoint in Public Digital Technologies and the New Morphology of Demonstration," *Theory, Culture & Society* 25, no. 5 (2008): 30–55.

31. Knoblauch, "The Performance of Knowledge," 75.

32. Ibid., 80.

33. Ibid., 92.

6. THE POWER OF CONSULTANTS

1. Here is one of the best known witticisms about consultants: "A consultant is someone who consults your watch, tells you the time, and charges for the service."

2. See Paul Bouffartigue and Charles Gadéa, "Les ingénieurs français: Spécificités nationales et dynamiques récentes d'un groupe professionnel," *Revue française de sociologie* 38, no. 2 (1997): 301–26.

3. Valérie Boussard, "Les consultants au coeur des interdépendances de l'espace de la gestion," *Cahiers internationaux de sociologie* 126 (2009): 99–113.

4. Olivier Babeau, "Les pratiques transgressives des consultants au service de la fabrique de la stratégie," *Revue française de gestion* 174 (2007): 43–59. Valérie Boussard has this to say: "Consultants . . . develop new models and tools and construct material and discursive presentations that make it possible to transform this technical knowledge into a commercial offering. . . . These engineers define themselves as scientists concerned with bringing scientific method and scientific thinking into business." Boussard, "Les consultants," 101.

5. Michel Armatte and Amy Dahan Dalmedico, "Modèles et Modélisations 1950–2000: Nouvelles pratiques, nouveaux enjeux," *Revue d'histoire des sciences* 57, no. 2 (2004): 245.

6. Notably in the work of Jan Tinbergen: "The first mathematical modeling of the economy, identified as the 'marginalist revolution' that established the neoclassical school, was marked by a strong analogy with mechanics in its concepts (reductionism) and in its formalism (linear algebra and differential calculus) at the very time physics was leaving this paradigm behind." Ibid., 251.

7. Operational research (also known as decision support) provides conceptual models to analyze complex situations, work out the best decisions, and enable decision makers to make the most effective choices.

8. On the subject of "information culture" more generally, it is worth consulting Armand Mattelart, *Histoire de la société de l'information* (Paris: La Découverte, 2001), 35–41, where one discovers the essential role of the former mathematician, Harvard professor, and president of Ford, Robert McNamara, in the rationalization of management in the Kennedy administration, where he was secretary of defense during the Cuban missile crisis and the beginnings of the Vietnam War. The American sociologist Daniel Bell names in the pantheon of figures inspiring technocracy Henri de Saint-Simon, Frederick Taylor, and Robert McNamara.

9. See, for example, www.slideshare.net, http://presentationload .com, http://thepowerpointtemplates.com.

10. Some ironically decipher the acronym as please don't change anything, to demonstrate that quality has already been achieved.

11. After founding the Boston Consulting Group in 1963, Bruce Henderson soon demonstrated his intention to make BCG a point of reference by providing scientific foundations to strategy, creating models taught to all MBA students: "The reputation of BCG in the business world from the beginning was that it was an innovative firm, able to create its own concepts and tools. Over the years, BCG's theories about competition and approaches to stra-

tegic problems were adopted by business schools throughout the
world. . . . BCG's clients still turn to the firm for its creativity
and its apparent objectivity based on scientific rationality." Frédéric
Leroy and Estelle Pellegrin-Boucher, "Bruce Henderson comme
fondateurs de la pensée stratégique," *Revue française de gestion* 154
(2005): 9–20.

12. In 2000, he was honored with the title of university professor at Harvard.

13. See Éric Maton, "Représentation graphique et pensée managériale: Le cas de la *Harvard Business Review* de 1922 à 1999," dissertation, École Polytechnique, Paris, 1977, p. 277.

14. These large firms also have other means of distribution:
journals, schools, media, conferences, and so on.

15. Firms often subcontract in the United States to take advantage of the time difference, which makes it possible to produce
slides the night before a presentation.

16. See http://office.microsoft.com.

17. www.slideshare.net and http://modeles-powerpoint.blogspot
.com.

18. See http://slideshop.com.

7. UNIVERSAL CONTAMINATION

1. David Stark and Verena Paravel, "PowerPoint in Public
Digital Technologies and the New Morphology of Demonstration,"
Theory, Culture & Society 25, no. 5 (2008): 30–55.

2. "Colin Powell on Iraq, Race, and Hurricane Relief," *20/20*,
ABC News, September 8, 2005, http://abcnews.go.com/2020/
Politics/story?id=1105979&page=1.

3. Philippe Quéau, "Les images et la guerre, ou *vidi vici*,"
Culture Technique 14 (1985): 225–37.

4. See Alexandre Pukall, "L'image militaire," 2002, www
.thehackademy.net/madchat/esprit/textes/illuminati/militaire.pdf.

5. See, for example, www.checkpoint-online.ch.

6. James Fallows, "Will Iran Be Next?" *The Atlantic*, December 2004, www.theatlantic.com/magazine/archive/2004/12/will-iran -be-next/3599.

7. This former air force colonel had conducted maneuvers for twenty years at the National War College and many other military institutions. Starting two years before the first Gulf War, he created and ran at least fifty exercises involving an attack on Iraq.

8. Fallows, "Will Iran Be Next?"

9. Greg Jaffe, "A Camp Divided: As U.S. Tries to Give Iraqi Troops More Responsibility, Clash of Two American Colonels Shows Tough Road Ahead," *Wall Street Journal*, June 16, 2006.

10. Thomas Ricks, *Fiasco: The American Military Adventure in Iraq* (New York: Penguin, 2006), 75.

11. Particularly retired Major Andrew J. Bacevich in his book *The New American Militarism* (New York: Oxford University Press, 2005).

12. Elisabeth Bumiller, "We Have Met the Enemy and He Is PowerPoint," *New York Times*, April 26, 2010.

13. Ibid. This is a forum for American company commanders, http://companycommand.army.mil/index.htm.

14. See www.pptclasses.com. See also a PowerPoint gallery intended for the military, www.armystudyguide.com.

15. Tyler E. Woodridge, "Nobody Asked Me, But . . . Order a PowerPoint Stand-Down," U.S. Naval Institute, *Proceedings*, December 2004, www.military.com/NewContent/0,13190,NI _1204_PowerPoint,00.html.

16. This was the case after the September 2001 attacks, when the CIA was accused of relying too heavily on its technological resources.

17. Bumiller, "We Have Met the Enemy and He Is Power-Point."

18. Gregory S. Pece, "The PowerPoint Society: The Influence

of PowerPoint in the U.S. Government and Bureaucracy," masters thesis, Virginia Polytechnic Institute, 2005, p. 61, http://scholar .lib.vt.edu/theses/available/etd-05202005-065041/unrestricted /PecePPthesis.pdf.

19. Marie-Josée Kotlicki and Jean-François Bolzinger, *Pour en finir avec le Wall Street Management* (Paris: L'Atelier, 2009).

20. Claire Guélaud, "Les Français se plaignent d'une dégradation des services publics," *Le Monde*, March 3, 2010.

21. The Budget Minister at the time, Eric Woerth, was a former employee of Accenture (formerly Arthur Andersen). It can be presumed that he was not totally unfamiliar with missions of this kind.

22. In managerial newspeak, "high impact" is a cost often connected to "human resources."

23. Denis Saint-Martin, "Le consulting et l'État: Une analyse comparée de l'offre et de la demande," *Revue française d'administration publique* 120 (2006): 743.

24. Ibid., 744.

25. Ibid., 746.

26. Instituted by the "Soisson" law of August 2, 1989, the social plan was renamed the job-saving plan by the law for social modernization of January 17, 2002. The expression *social plan* was already a euphemism (for mass layoffs). The job-saving plan is a procedure incumbent on the employer that applies to companies with more than fifty employees when the layoffs contemplated are at least ten in number. Intended to limit layoffs, the PSE has to offer alternative measures, such as transfer, reduction in hours, and so on, as well as a "placement" plan.

27. Paula Cristofalo, "L'institutionnalisation d'une fonction d'expertise et de conseil auprès des élus du personnel," *Cahiers internationaux de sociologie* 126 (2009).

28. Ibid.

29. The rather crass head of the company at the time, Didier

Lombard, finally speaking publicly after twenty suicides, called it a fad. The term and his bad management of the crisis cost him his job a few months later. See Ivan Du Roy, *Orange stressé* (Paris: La Découverte, 2009).

30. See Lucie Delaporte, "Le clin deuil de France Telecom à ses salariés," September 15, 2009, www.bakchich.info/Le-clin-deuil -de-France-Telecom-a,08691.html.

31. See www.orgaconsultants.com.

32. Mobility is one of the key values of contemporary entre-preneurial ideology. Many companies require their employees to move every four or five years. To meet the needs of the contem-porary company, an employee must be able to adapt to any new role or function to which she is assigned. Expertise and experience no longer are primary values. What counts is the ability to join in projects.

33. Another remarkable example of euphemism.

34. Delaporte, "Le clin deuil de France Telecom à ses salariés."

8. AT SCHOOL WITH POWERPOINT?

1. Who inspired the neoliberal policies of Margaret Thatcher in Great Britain and Ronald Reagan in the United States.

2. See http://nobelprize.org/nobel_prizes/economics/laureates /1992.

3. "The main aim of the framework is to support Member States in further developing their educational and training systems. These systems should better provide the means for all citizens to realize their potentials, as well as ensure sustainable economic pros-perity and employability." Conclusions of the European Council, May 12, 2009, on a strategic framework for European cooperation in education and training, http://europa.eu/legislation_summaries /education_training_youth/general_framework/ef0016_en.htm.

4. Ministry of Labor, 2009.

5. Proposed Finance Law 2010, Ministry of Labor Web site, www.travail-emploi-sante.gouv.fr.

6. Since the explosion of the Web, the question of the effectiveness of training in terms of cost and speed has led companies to turn toward virtual training programs via computer, no longer requiring the presence of a trainer. This vogue of e-learning and online apprenticeship has begun to take root in several sectors.

7. These studies proliferated from 2005 on. In addition to those cited elsewhere, see Dale Cyphert, "The Problem of PowerPoint: Visual Aid or Visual Rhetoric?" *Business Communication Quarterly* 67, no. 1 (March 2004): 80–84; Jens E. Kjeldsen, "The Rhetoric of PowerPoint," *International Journal of Media, Technology and Lifelong Learning* (www.seminar.net) 2, no. 1 (2006); James Katt et al., "Establishing Best Practices for the Use of PowerPoint as a Presentation Aid," *Human Communication* 11, no. 2 (2008): 189–96.

8. See David K. Farkas, "Toward a Better Understanding of PowerPoint Deck Design," *Information Design Journal + Document Design* 14, no. 2 (2006): 162–71.

9. David K. Farkas, "A Heuristic for Reasoning About PowerPoint Deck Design," International Professional Communications Conference, Montreal, July 13–16, 2008, http://faculty.washington.edu/farkas/Farkas-PowerPointHeuristic.pdf.

10. In addition to Ian Parker, "Absolute PowerPoint: Can a Software Package Edit Our Thoughts?" *New Yorker*, May 28, 2001, see: Clive Thompson, "PowerPoint Makes You Dumb," *New York Times*, December 14, 2003; John Naughton, "How PowerPoint Can Fatally Weaken Your Argument," *Observer*, December 21, 2003; and Julia Keller, "Is PowerPoint the Devil?" *Chicago Tribune*, January 22, 2003.

11. David G. Levasseur and J. Kanan Sawyer, "Pedagogy Meets PowerPoint: A Research Review of the Effects of Computer-Generated Slides in the Classroom," *Review of Communication* 6 (2006): 101–23.

12. Russell Craig and Joel Amernic, "PowerPoint Presentation Technology and the Dynamics of Teaching," *Innovative Higher Education* 31 (2006): 150.

13. *Business Communication Quarterly*, for example, published articles and special issues on the use of PowerPoint in March and June 2004, in December 2006, and in December 2007.

14. Satoshi Suhagara and Gregory Boland, "The Effectiveness of PowerPoint Presentations in the Accounting Classroom," *Accounting Education* 15, no. 4 (December 2006): 391–403.

15. Ibid.

16. Wim Blokzijl and Roos Naeff, "The Instructor as Stagehand: Dutch Student Responses to PowerPoint," *Business Communication Quarterly* 67 (2004): 76, 71.

17. Nicole Amare, "To Slideware or Not to Slideware: Students' Experiences with PowerPoint vs. Lecture," *Journal of Technical Writing and Communication* 36 (2006): 302.

18. Ted Simons, "Does PowerPoint Make You Stupid?" *Presentations*, Mar. 2004, 26.

19. See http://media.enseignementsup-recherche.gouv.fr/file/Rapport_CDHSS/33/8/CDHSS-version14janvier2010remiserapport_133338.pdf.

20. Relying on a 2004 CEREQ study according to which the rate of unemployment for *licenciés* in HSS was 8.4 percent compared to 7.5 percent overall, www.cereq.fr.

21. Its dominance is truly universal. Referring to the Party School in China, for example: "All classrooms are equipped to enable lecturers to use PowerPoint, a practice followed by all professors in the School without exception, all of whom have taken a training program for that purpose. . . . Presenting one's class on PowerPoint slides has become the guarantee of teaching that is both professional and up to date." Émilie Tran, "École du Parti et formation des élites dirigeantes en Chine," *Cahiers internationales de sociologie* 122 (2007): 131.

22. Christian Laval, "La réforme managériale et sécuritaire de l'école," in *L'Appel des appels*, ed. Roland Gori, Barbara Cassin, and Christian Laval (Paris: Fayard, 2009), available online at www .mutations-institut-fsu.org/?p=274. See also Laval, "L'école saisie par l'utilitarisme," *Cités* 10 (2002): 63–74, and "Les deux crises de l'éducation," *Revue du MAUSS* 28 (2006): 96–115.

23. "The Definition and Selection of Key Competencies," www .oecd.org/dataoecd/47/61/35070367.pdf.

24. These three areas of competencies are the credo behind the checklists used by HR directors in companies, notably in writing guides for annual evaluation interviews.

25. "The Definition and Selection of Key Competencies."

26. Angélique del Rey, *À l'école des compétences: De l'éducation à la fabrique de l'élève performant* (Paris: La Découverte, 2010), 83.

27. See the work of Bertrand Schwartz, who was one of the major initiators of professional training in France.

28. Del Rey, *À l'école des compétences*, 74.

29. See "A Memorandum on Lifelong Learning," from the 2000 Lisbon summit meeting.

30. Lucie Tanguy, "De l'éducation à la formation: quelles réformes?" *Éducation et Sociétés* 16 (2005): 99–122.

31. In the front rank was the Institut Montaigne.

32. Tanguy, "De l'éducation à la formation."

33. Among the most complete of them are: www.lewebpeda gogique.com, www.cafepedagogique.net, www.cahiers-pedagogi ques.com, www.educnet.education.fr, and www.inattendu.org /grape.

34. Instituted by then Minister of Education Claude Allègre, the *travaux personnels encadrés* (TPE) are school research projects conducted by groups of two to four students in targeted areas of a particular set of questions. They are used in the senior classes of the general *lycées* and provide a foretaste of the baccalaureate exam.

35. Report of the Mission e-Educ on the development of digital technology in schools, May 2008, 11.

36. Ibid., 13.

37. The Web site of the Agency for the uses of TICE (Technologies de l'Information et de la Communication pour l'Enseignement), Information and Communication Technology in Education (ICTE), www.agence-usages-tice.education.fr, presents an anthology of laudatory studies of the IWB. It should be noted that most English public schools will have IWBs in 2012.

38. The Swiss education site Schooling in Switzerland provides a fairly complete survey on the IWB; see www.educa.ch.

39. Interview in *La Lettre des professionels de l'éducation*, November 2, 2009, http://education.weka.fr.

40. See www.educnet.education.fr.

41. Which presupposes from the start that in the home of every student attending a digital school there is access to a computer and to the Internet.

42. An intranet is a private computer network for a company or an institution, as the Internet is a public network for the world community of Web surfers.

43. The Ministry of Education site provides a map of deployment by academy in *lycées* and *collèges* in 2010, www.educnet.education .fr. For example, the state spent €67 million in 2009 to equip 6,700 rural schools with digital resources (source: www.education .gouv.fr).

44. Philippe Danino and Christian Laval, "Construire l'école transparente?" available at http://skhole.fr.

45. CREDOC studies and surveys of "les conditions de vie et les aspirations des Français" (2007).

46. We are living in a society that has considered detecting possible behavioral problems among very young children. See "Trouble des conduites chez l'enfant et l'adolescent," Institut National de la Santé et de la Recherche Médicale (INSERM), September 2005.

47. Danino and Laval, "Construire l'école transparente?"

CONCLUSION: THE PERVERSITY OF A SOFTWARE PROGRAM

1. "L'avenir est aux entreprises Y," *Enjeux-Les Échos*, June 2010.

2. Publicity by companies intended to demonstrate their commitment to sustainable development.

3. There are lists of prize companies where it's good to work.

4. On this question see the work of Bernard Stiegler, particularly *Réenchanter le monde* (Paris: Flammarion, 2006).

5. See Jeremy Rifkin, *The Age of Access* (New York: Putnam, 2000).

6. Ibid., 35.

7. Stéphane Lefrancq and Eric Maton, "Attention aux présentations qui tuent," *L'Expansion Management Review* 132 (2009): 48–59.

INDEX